THE PERFECT MARRIAGE

THE ART OF MATCHING FOOD & SHERRY WINES FROM JEREZ

SIMON &
SCHUSTER

LONDON · NEW YORK · SYDNEY · TORONTO

First published in Great Britain by
Simon & Schuster UK Ltd, 2007
A CBS COMPANY

13 5 7 9 10 8 6 4 2

Simon & Schuster UK Ltd,
Africa House,
64-78 Kingsway,
London WC2B 6AH

www.simonsays.co.uk

A CIP catalogue record for this book
is available from the British Library

ISBN-13: 9781847370037
ISBN-10: 1-84737-003-9

Designed by Fiona Andreanelli
Edited by Carey Denton
Photography by Sam Bailey
Photograph of Heston Blumenthal by Jose Lopez de Zubiria
Front Cover and Pages 1, 2, 7, 8, 9, 10-11, 12-13, 32, 38,
112-113 Alamy
Pages 36, 64, 88, 110, 138 Photography by Dan Duchars
With thanks to Kim Morphew, Neil Beckett and Fiona Simms

Printed in China

Acknowledgements
With special thanks to:
Bosco Torremocha – Director General of Fedejerez, the Association
of Sherry Shippers.
All of the sherry bodegas, and their Jerez and UK representatives
alike, for their unwavering support of the sherry and Ten Star
Tapas campaign over the past four years.
All of the chefs for being such passionate fans of sherry and
creating these wonderful recipes.

www.tenstartapas.com

CONTENTS

FOREWORD BY HESTON BLUMENTHAL

LIFE IS GEARED TO CONTRASTS AND OPPOSITES. THINK OF IT IN terms of film – the most dramatic scenes are when fear follows on from serenity. Likewise in food, the most exhilarating and enjoyable moments are often those when the contrast is at its greatest. So, within a mouthful, you might go from soft to crisp, or, in the case of a menu, where different flavours are followed by different textures.

That's the joy of tasting menus. Being served a succession of smaller, individual dishes that provide different flavours, smells, textures, temperatures and tastes avoids the dumbing down of the palate. Tasting menus not only stimulate the senses, they create a much more enjoyable experience overall.

In culinary terms, tasting is the polar opposite to the traditional three-course meal. While it's currently considered cutting edge in the UK, where the nearest equivalent would be bar snacks such as devils on horseback or scotch eggs served in village pubs, there's

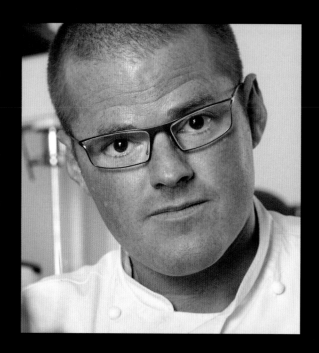

> **"**Sherry is the traditional wine to drink with tapas, and its complexity and huge range of styles also makes it a perfect wine partner for tasting.**"**

nothing new in the concept itself. The small portions and strong social emphasis inherent to tasting are also found in the culinary traditions of many different cultures, from the food stalls and vendors in the streets of South East Asia, Egypt and India, to the souks and bazaars of Morocco.

In Europe, this approach to food is most famously found in the tapas bars of Spain. For tasting, as with tapas, pairing and partnering these foods with wines is an integral part of the experience. Wine becomes as important as the food in the way it can help to add to the enjoyment of the taste, and can highlight the different notes of flavours in the cuisine. That's why matching wines within the context of a tasting menu is so vital — it helps to continue the rhythm of the meal and adds to the menu's balance.

Sherry is the traditional wine to drink with tapas, and its complexity and huge range of styles also makes it a perfect wine partner for tasting. Because it delivers in the mid-tongue acidity area, it really does make food perceptibly juicier — it quite literally whets the appetite. So sherry can genuinely enhance the appeal of all foods.

I was first introduced to sherry about 15 years ago by a man called Lance Falstaff at Harringdon Wine Company in Thame. It was a revelation, and about eight years ago I held a lunch for wine writers at *The Fat Duck* where I created seven dishes to accompany my favourite sherry styles. One of the dishes was sweetbreads cooked in hay, and wrapped in salt crust pastry with herbs, which acts like a hermetic seal. It was served with braised lettuce with clams, and washed back with an aged VOS Oloroso, which went with it fantastically well. Following that, I introduced a page at the front of the wine menu offering thirty different sherries by the glass. At the time it was a first for this country, but I wanted to make sure people knew we were taking it seriously.

In Spain, and especially Jerez where it originates, sherry has always been respected as a fine and versatile wine that can partner many different dishes. Like all wines, it has a huge variety of complexities of balance and flavour, and indeed strengths. That's why some sherries work well with more robust dishes, such as the marinated fish and spicy garlic chorizo that are found in tapas bars throughout Spain, while other varieties of sherry are better suited to lighter, more subtle dishes. Cream sherry and fois gras are terrific together, as is manzanilla and sardines. Amontillado pairs well with pecorino, and on a hot summer's day a good fino is a must with some salty anchovies or nuts. The range of sherry styles is so vast that it can perfectly partner virtually every type of food.

As part of my research into pairing sherry styles with both everyday and more obscure, globally sourced ingredients, I focused on the fifth taste, umami. The other four tastes are sweet, sour, salty and bitter, while umami, which was first discovered in Japan, is the taste of the common food flavouring, monosodium glutamate. It occurs naturally in certain foods, and sherry also has special umami properties which lend it to both everyday and way-out ingredients. My research indicates that certain taste compounds that are found in sherry are also present in foods such as tomatoes, seafood and some meats, so it makes perfect sense that it has a role to play in uncovering this exciting new area of food science.

We are really only just beginning to scratch the surface of taste and flavour, but sherry genuinely encourages our receptivity to food, which makes it an ideal wine to accompany tasting. If you look at sherry and food matching like a continually evolving film or novel, you can understand why so many leading names in gastronomy — as this book shows — choose it as a partner for their menus.

INTRODUCTION

> **"If I had a thousand sons, the first human principle I would teach them — would be to forswear thin potations and dedicate themselves to sack sherry."**
>
> William Shakespeare (Henry IV, Part II)

SHERRY HAS LONG BEEN RECOGNISED BY THOSE WHO APPRECIATE food and wine as one of the world's finest and most versatile wines. *The Perfect Marriage* sees fifteen of the UK's top chefs celebrate their love for sherry and food matching; contributing recipes that reflect their cultural backgrounds, interests, influences and their passion for sherry. The result is a collection of tasting menus drawn from culinary traditions around the world including Japan, India, 'fusion', traditional English, British Asian, Spanish and Australasian.

Chefs who love food have always loved sherry and its versatility has earned it a place on the world's finest wine lists at the world's finest restaurants. This acceptance has seen drinking sherry with food being adopted at dinner tables all over the country, and this book is your guide to sherry and food pairing.

Complex, stylish and unexpected: sherries should be drunk just like wine, not stored away for months or years and imbibed by the thimbleful! Sherry Styles (see page 10) gives a clear definition of each sherry, its flavour characteristics and how best to serve it,

with a gallery of recommendations for the sherry novice. As Heston Blumenthal asserts, the diversity of sherry styles ensures a perfect match for virtually any ingredient and he makes his top ten sherry and ingredients pairings (see page 50).

To demonstrate how utterly versatile sherry is, there are specific pairing recommendations for every recipe. From the unexpected sweetness of a cream sherry served with spicy Indian cooking, to a brisk, sharp fino or manzanilla to accompany the freshest fish found in Japanese dishes, to the rich mellow notes of Pedro Ximénez to accompany mouth-watering desserts. Sweet oloroso or moscatel are paired with tangy blue cheese and dry amontillado with that most British of ingredients: offal. A nutty palo cortado carries the flavour of slow-roast lamb and a sweet but light pale cream matches perfectly with salt cod.

Whatever your food or drink preferences the recipes, menus and sherry pairing recommendations will bring an exciting new eating experience to your table. Enjoy!

JEREZ, XÉRÈZ, SHERRY -
A WINE SO GOOD THEY NAMED IT THREE TIMES

Throw away those timid little glasses that come out once a year, and instead savour the delights of chilled sherry in a good-sized wine glass.

TAKE NOTE, SHERRY IS ONLY SHERRY IF IT COMES FROM THE JEREZ region in Andalucía in south-west Spain. And the best come from the 'sherry triangle', the region defined by the three towns of Jerez de la Frontera, Sanlúcar de Barrameda and El Puerto de Santa María, where the wines mature in bodegas.

The principal grape used for sherry is palomino, a white variety accounting for 95 per cent of production. Almost everywhere else in the world, it's a pretty unremarkable variety. Only here does it produce really special results, where it undergoes a magical metamorphosis into sherry.

Despite the many different styles there are basically two groups of palomino sherries: fino and manzanilla, both pale and bone dry; and amontillado and oloroso, mahogany-coloured and concentrated. All are naturally dry, but depending on how they are aged, treated and mixed they produce all the other styles.

In the creation of a fine sherry – unlike most other wines – where and how the grapes are grown is not as important as where and how the wine is made. The two key elements are ageing and – as in other fine wines such as champagne and port – blending. The 'where', the wine-making itself, takes place at the bodegas, the cathedral-like warehouses scattered across the region, positioned specifically to

attract the sea breezes or humidity needed to mature the wines. The 'how' involves the secret ingredient 'flor' and the mixing of younger and older wines by the solera system.

Fino and manzanilla owe their special tangy character to flor (literally 'flower'), a bread-like yeast that grows on the wine when it's stored in old butts (barrels). The growth of flor varies according to the type of wine being made — it's

> **"The two key elements are ageing and — as in other fine wines such as champagne and port — blending."**

thickest in manzanilla and less vigorous in fino, and killed off completely in amontillado and oloroso, which are fortified to a higher strength of around 18 per cent alcohol (flor dies at 16 per cent and above).

Then, in addition to flor, there is the solera system, an accelerated ageing process that allows the older wines to impart their qualities to the younger ones. When sherry is needed for bottling, a little is removed from the oldest barrels, which is replaced with an equal amount from the next oldest barrels, and so on back to the youngest. The young wines gain a complexity and intensity they wouldn't otherwise show and the consistency, quality and style of the wine is ensured.

Finally, the stylistic range is widened further by blending, colouring and sweetening. There are two other grape varieties used in sherry making: muscat and Pedro Ximénez. Both are used to sweeten other sherries to make pale cream, medium and cream, as well as sweetened amontillado and oloroso. However, they also produce wines in their own right, moscatel and the sensationally dark and rich Pedro Ximénez. Genuine palo cortado is something special too, as it starts life as a fino but then the flor dies away and it matures as an oloroso.

The sherry spectrum is indeed so wide, from the driest, finest and lightest, to the heaviest, richest and sweetest, that there is no more versatile wine in the world.

LEFT: Pouring fino using a venencia, a long-handled ladle that allows sherry to be drawn from the barrel without disturbing the flor.
TOP: Flor grows on fino and manzanilla as it is stored in barrels.
TOP RIGHT: The chalky soil of Jerez clings to the little rain that falls.
ABOVE RIGHT: Palomino grapes undergo a magical metamorphosis to produce wonderful sherry.

SHERRY STYLES

MANZANILLA A delicate style of fino made only in Sanlúcar. Pale. Appley, salty, yeasty nose. Dry, with a very light body (normally only 15 per cent alcohol by volume), and a tangy, zesty finish. Manzanilla pasada has additional age, giving more body and complexity. Storage and serving as for fino. Among the finest are La Goya, La Guita, Barbadillo's Solear, Argüeso's Las Medallas and Pasada San Léon, Hidalgo's La Gitana and superb, single-vineyard Pasada Pastrana, and the outstanding Lustau Almacenista wines. Served well chilled. Once open, should be stored in the fridge and drunk within two or three weeks.

FINO Pale. 'Elegant' (as the name suggests) and fresh on the nose, with hints of almonds. Dry, with a light body and crisp finish. Among the best are Harvey's Fino, Domecq's La Ina, González-Byass' Tio Pepe, Lustau's Puerto Fino, Osborne's Fino Quinta, José de Soto's Fino and Valdespino's exceptional, single-vineyard Inocente. Storage and serving as for Manzanilla.

AMONTILLADO An aged fino, from which the flor has died away. Amber of different shades, depending on age (up to 60 years). Gently pungent, hazelnutty. Light to medium body. Naturally dry, but available sweetened. Serve lightly chilled. Once open, only finer, older wines should be left for more than two or three months. In addition to brands like Harveys Club Classic and Sandeman's Dry Don try Domecq's ancient Amontillado 51-1A (VORS), Valdespino's intense Coliseo (VORS) and González Byass' Del Duque (VORS).

OLOROSO Amber to mahogany. 'Fragrant' bouquet (hence the name), walnutty. Medium-full body, smooth texture. Naturally dry, but marketed in both dry and sweeter styles.

Among the former, seek out Barbadillo's Cuco (VORS), Pedro Romero's Viña El Alamo (VORS), Lustau's Almacenista Pata de Gallina, and Williams & Humbert's Solera Especial (15 Year Old). Among the latter, Barbadillo's San Rafael (VORS), González Byass' Matusalem (VORS), Sandeman's Royal Corregidor (VOS) and Domecq's Sibarita (VORS).

PALO CORTADO Genuine palo cortado is a wine which appeared to be developing as a fino, but from which the flor died away and which aged as an oloroso. Commercial palo cortado is a blend of amontillado and oloroso. Known as Jerez cortado when made in Sanlúcar. Bright mahogany. Delicate and hazelnutty on the nose; rich, round and smooth on the palate. Serve at room temperature. Greats are González Byass' Apóstoles (VORS), Hidalgo's Jerez Cortado, Williams & Humbert's Solera Especial (20 Year Old) and Colosia's Palo Cortado Viejisimo.

A few simple facts will help you choose the right sherry for the occasion. Explore, experiment…and most of all, enjoy!

PALE CREAM A sweetened fino. Pale. Some fino character on the nose. Light-medium body and medium-sweet palate. Almost biscuity. Serve well chilled as a refreshing late morning aperitif. Among the most available are Croft Original and Harveys Pale Cream. Also experiment with Emilio Lustau's Finest Pale Cream Sherry, Hidalgo's Pale Cream and those from Barbadillo and De Soto.

MEDIUM A sweetened oloroso, although it is sometimes labelled medium-dry. Also known by traditional terms such as brown, golden, milk or rich. Amber to mahogany. Medium body and sweetness. Serve lightly chilled or as a warming aperitif on a cold day. After fino, medium is the second most-consumed sherry in the world, having a huge market in Germany and Holland. Try Dry Sack Medium, Osborne's Medium and Osborne's Rich Golden.

CREAM A sweetened amontillado or oloroso. Amber to mahogany. Rich aroma, full body, and round, smooth texture. Sweet. Serve lightly chilled or even on the rocks with a slice of orange as an aperitif. The best-known brand is Harveys Bristol Cream. Among many others are those from Barbadillo, Colosía, De Soto, Don Zoilo, Delgado Zuleta, Lustau Reservas Capataz Andres and Superior, and Williams & Humbert's Canasta Cream.

MOSCATEL (MUSCAT) One of the other two grape varieties used for sherry. Normally used to sweeten other sherries, but also a remarkable wine in its own right, made from sun-dried grapes. Mahogany colour. Pronounced raisiny nose and palate. Medium-full body, smooth texture. Sweet. Serve at room temperature. Among the best are Lustau's Reserva Superior Emilin and those from Colosía, Pedro Romero and Delgado Zuleta.

PEDRO XIMÉNEZ (PX) A grape variety used to colour and sweeten other sherries and to make a unique wine from sun-dried grapes. Dark mahogany. Pungent nose of caramel and raisins. Full body, luxuriantly rich, round, thick and velvety. Very sweet. Serve at room temperature. Try Colosía, Don Zoilo, Pedro Romero, Delgado Zuleta, Sánchez Romate and Valdespino. The finest include González Byass' Noé (VORS), Williams & Humbert's Solera Especial (20 Year Old), Lustau's centenary bottling Murillo, and Domecq's suitably named Venerable (VORS).

AGE-DATED SHERRIES VOS are officially recognised as being more than 20 years old; VORS more than 30.

SKYE GYNGELL

SKYE GYNGELL IS HEAD CHEF AT THE AWARD-WINNING *Petersham Nurseries Café* and food writer for both *Vogue* (UK) and *The Independent on Sunday Review*. She is passionate about food and passionate, too, about choosing the right sherry to accompany her dishes. Excited by the choice and complexity of sherries available, she also enjoys incorporating sherry into her recipes.

Skye was raised in Australia and worked at a number of Sydney's culinary institutions before flying to Paris to complete her formal training under Anne Willan at La Varenne. After a stint at the *Dodin-Bouffant* in Paris, Skye moved to London to work at *The French House* and, notably, *The Dorchester* with Anton Mossiman.

"Sherry is such a broad term. From the driest to the sweetest styles, they can be so different and when paired with food offer such a heavenly experience. For example, a crisp, dry manzanilla would go wonderfully with really cold crab and mayonnaise, cutting through the rich, sweet seafood and a bone-dry fino would work with a dish of clams."

PAN-FRIED SQUID WITH WHITE POLENTA AND SHERRY SAUCE

Best paired with:
FINO

THIS IDEA COMES FROM THE PAIRING OF *FRITTO MISTO DI MARE* (MIXED FRIED SEAFOOD) and soft polenta seen so frequently in Venice and the surrounding area. White polenta has a complex flavour, yet at the same time is richer and mellower than the more common yellow polenta. The seafood and polenta are married together with the sherry butter. Serve with a chilled wine glass of fino. If you are short on time you can use instant quick cook yellow polenta instead.

PREPARATION AND COOKING TIME: **50 MINUTES**   SERVES **4**

500 ml cold water | 200 g white polenta | 215 g unsalted butter, cold and diced | 2 tablespoons good quality sherry vinegar | 4 tablespoons fino sherry | 1 shallot, finely chopped | 6 black peppercorns | a sprig of fresh thyme | 1 tablespoon mild olive oil | 4 prepared young squid, cleaned | salt and black pepper, to season

1 Put the water in a pan and bring to a simmer. Stir in the polenta and continue to stir until the water returns to a simmer. Reduce the heat until the polenta only occasionally splutters and cook for 40 minutes, stirring occasionally until thickened. Stir in 40 g butter and season to taste.

2 Meanwhile, put the sherry vinegar, sherry, shallot, peppercorns and thyme into a small pan. Cook over a medium heat until reduced down to no more than a tablespoon. Pass through a sieve and return the liquid to a clean pan. Over a medium heat whisk in the remaining butter piece by piece until the sauce is smooth and thickened. Season to taste. Set aside and keep warm.

3 Just before the polenta is ready, heat the oil in a non-stick pan over a high heat. Season the squid generously with salt and black pepper. When the oil is smoking, add the squid and cook without turning for 1 minute. Turn over the squid and cook for a further minute on the other side until golden.

4 To serve, spoon the polenta on to a plate, pile the squid on top and pour over the sherry butter.

POACHED CHERRIES & GOAT'S CHEESE SALAD WITH PARMA HAM

Best paired with:
MANZANILLA

WHO COULD RESIST FRESH, RIPE, SWEET CHERRIES AND TANGY YOUNG GOAT'S CHEESE combined with Parma ham followed by a glass of manzanilla? To make a real difference use good quality honey and look for one made locally to your area, by local bees! Be adventurous and experiment with salad leaves: why not try beet tops, white dandelion, basil, mint, chervil and wild rocket?

PREPARATION AND COOKING TIME: **45 MINUTES** SERVES **4**

1 generous tablespoon good quality honey | 75 ml dry sherry such as manzanilla or fino | 150 g fresh cherries | 1 red onion, cut into 3 mm thick rounds | 4 tablespoons balsamic vinegar | 5 tablespoons extra virgin olive oil | 1 tablespoon sugar | 1 teaspoon Dijon mustard | 1 teaspoon lemon juice | about 100 g mixed salad leaves | 12 slices Parma ham | 300 g soft young goat's cheese | 75 g toasted hazelnuts, roughly chopped | 1 tablespoon finely chopped curly leaf parsley | sea-salt and freshly ground black pepper, to season

1 Preheat the oven to Gas Mark 4/180°C/350°F. Put the honey and sherry into a saucepan and gently heat until the honey has melted. Add the cherries and remove from the heat. Allow to cool. Reserve 1 tablespoon of the liquid and set aside.

2 Put the onion on a baking tray and pour over the balsamic vinegar and 2 tablespoons olive oil. Sprinkle with the sugar and season with a little salt and pepper. Roast in the oven for 25 minutes, turning once. Allow to cool.

3 Meanwhile, make a dressing by mixing the mustard, lemon juice and reserved cherry syrup in a bowl. Slowly whisk in the remaining oil, check the seasoning and set aside.

4 Place the salad leaves in a bowl and toss lightly with a couple of teaspoons of dressing. Divide among four plates.

5 To serve, layer the salad starting with a slice of Parma ham, a crumbling of goat's cheese, some red onions and a cherry or two. Repeat until you have used everything up. Scatter over the hazelnuts, drizzle the remaining dressing and finally sprinkle over the parsley.

"Manzanilla reduced with honey and served with cheese is magical."

ROQUEFORT & FENNEL
STACKS WITH SHERRY SYRUP

Best paired with:
PALO CORTADO,
CREAM,
MOSCATEL

CHEESE AND HONEY IS SOMETHING SPECIAL, BUT BLUE CHEESE AND SHERRY IS earth–shatteringly good. This light grazing dish combines salty blue cheese with clean, cooling fennel and its perfect companion is sweet oloroso or moscatel. Any blue cheese works well, from the more delicate Dolcelatte, to English Stilton or the very strong Spanish blue cheeses such as Picon or Cabrales.

PREPARATION: **20 MINUTES**   SERVES **4**

2 tablespoons honey | 125 ml fino sherry | 250 g blue cheese, finely sliced | 1 large fennel bulb, outer leaves removed and really finely sliced

1 Heat the honey and sherry in a small saucepan over a medium heat. Bring to a simmer, then increase the heat and cook for 3–4 minutes until syrupy. Remove from the heat and allow to go cold.

2 To serve, divide amongst four plates: put a little of the cheese on a plate and top with a little fennel. Continue to layer up until all is used. Spoon over the sherry syrup and serve.

MOSCATEL

TASTING NOTES With a mahogany colour and strong caramel nose, medium – to full-bodied Moscatel has a smooth raisiny taste. **SERVING TEMPERATURE** Room temperature **FOOD** Fruit, dried fruits, blue cheeses, chocolate and traditional and rich puddings.

"I've found experimenting with sherry completely absorbing. It's so different to wine. Sherry lends a much more spicy depth and complexity."

GUINEA FOWL WITH MEDJOOL DATES

Best paired with:
AMONTILLADO,
DRY OLOROSO,
PALO CORTADO

THIS DISH HAS A SUBTLE, DELICIOUS GAMEY FLAVOUR AND A RICH SWEETNESS FROM THE Medjool dates. Serve with a glass of dry oloroso sherry. If you don't have a wide saucepan that can go in the oven, use a roasting pan on the hob instead.

PREPARATION AND COOKING TIME: **40 MINUTES**   SERVES **2–4**

1.5 kg guinea fowl, cut into 6 portions | 1 tablespoon mild olive oil | 5 bay leaves | 1 cinnamon stick, broken in half | 3 whole cloves | 125 ml Madeira wine | a wide strip of orange zest | a wide strip of lemon zest | 120 ml chicken stock | 10 Medjool dates, halved and stoned | salt and black pepper, to season

1 Preheat the oven to Gas Mark 6/200°C/ 400°F. Season the guinea fowl with lots of salt and black pepper.

2 Heat the olive oil in an ovenproof non-stick frying pan. When the oil is sizzling, arrange the pieces of guinea fowl in a single layer skin side down in the pan and cook for 5 minutes until the skin is browned. Remove from the heat and drain away nearly all of the fat.

3 Turn the guinea fowl over and tuck the bay leaves, cinnamon and cloves in between the pieces, then transfer to the middle of the oven for 8–10 minutes until just cooked. Remove the guinea fowl from the pan, lightly cover with foil and allow to stand.

4 Meanwhile, drain away any excess fat and return the pan to a high heat. Pour in the Madeira, orange and lemon zest, and scrape the sides and the base of the pan with a wooden spoon. Bring to the boil, reduce the heat and add the chicken stock and dates. Cook for 5 minutes, stirring until the sauce has thickened. Check seasoning and remove from the heat.

5 Arrange the pieces of roasted guinea fowl on a plate and spoon the sauce over the top.

WHITE PEACH & SHERRY ICE CREAM

Best paired with:
CREAM,
PEDRO XIMÉNEZ

NOTHING BEATS HOME-MADE ICE CREAM, AND THIS IS NO EXCEPTION. ENJOY A GENEROUS scoop in a bowl with a glass of chilled, velvety Pedro Ximénez.

PREPARATION AND COOKING TIME: **45 MINUTES, PLUS FREEZING**   SERVES **4–6**

300 ml organic full fat milk | 300 ml double cream | 2 vanilla pods, split in half lengthways | 4 organic free-range egg yolks | 225 g caster sugar | 200 ml cold water | 2 white peaches, halved and stoned | 2 tablespoons PX sherry

1 Gently heat the milk, cream and one vanilla pod in a heavy-based saucepan just to a simmer. Remove from the heat and allow to infuse for 10 minutes.

2 Meanwhile, beat the egg yolks and 125 g sugar together until light and pale. Stir in the warm milk mixture. Return the custard to the pan and cook over the lowest possible heat, stirring using a wooden spoon in a figure of eight motion, dragging the spoon along the base of the pan until the custard begins to thicken and clings to the back of the spoon. Remove from the heat, strain through a sieve and set aside to cool completely.

3 Put the water, remaining sugar and vanilla pod into a wide heavy-based saucepan and bring to a simmer. Lay the peach halves in the sugar syrup and poach for 5 minutes until soft. Remove from the heat and let the peaches cool completely in the syrup.

4 Once cool, strain the peaches and whiz in a blender with the sherry to make a smooth purée. Stir into the cooled custard. Pour into an ice cream maker and churn according to the manufacturer's instructions. Remove from the freezer 15 minutes before serving.

TIP If you don't have an ice cream maker, freeze in a sealable container until a thick edge of the ice cream is frozen. Then scrape into a food processor and whiz for a few seconds. Freeze again and repeat this process 3 more times, to remove all the ice crystals. Then freeze until solid.

"In some instances I've experimented by substitution and have been excited by the results; a beurre blanc with sherry, for example."

FERGUS HENDERSON

FERGUS HENDERSON TRAINED AS AN ARCHITECT BEFORE becoming a chef. He opened the *French House Dining Room* in 1992, and left in 1994 to start *St John Bread & Wine*. Set in a former smokehouse near Smithfield market, the restaurant revels in the rural British tradition of using every part of the animal.

Fergus Henderson's motto is 'nose to tail eating', and in this respect there is an affinity with traditional Spanish tapas. In Spain, it seems, they never learned to shun the less expensive but, as proved by Henderson's innovative creativity, equally delicious parts of the animal. These recipes use quintessentially British ingredients to create a tasting menu for those who like to eat on the wild side.

PIG'S HEAD WITH BEANS

Best paired with:
AMONTILLADO,
PALO CORTADO,
PEDRO XIMÉNEZ

COOKING A PIG'S HEAD WHOLE MAY SOUND CHALLENGING, BUT THE END RESULTS ARE well worth the effort of sourcing a pig's head – and the method of cooking is really quite straightforward. The comfort derived from pig's head and beans seems to embrace a lightly chilled glass of palo cortado. You could use a shoulder of pork if the pig's head is too scary.

PREPARATION AND COOKING TIME: 5½ HOURS   SERVES 6

1 pig's head or shoulder of pork, halved | 16 whole shallots | 12 garlic cloves | a bundle of thyme and rosemary sprigs | 125 ml brandy | 900 ml chicken stock | 200 g dried butter beans, soaked overnight | 1–2 tablespoons Dijon mustard | a handful of fresh chopped parsley | salt and black pepper, to season

1 Preheat the oven to Gas Mark 5/150°C/ 300°F. Put the pig's head in a large roasting tray with the shallots, 10 garlic cloves and thyme and rosemary.

2 Pour over the brandy and chicken stock and bring to the boil. Take off the heat and season the pig's head. Cover with foil. Place in the oven and cook gently for 4 hours.

3 Allow to cool in the cooking liquor. When cold enough to handle remove all the meat and reserve the cooking liquor, garlic and shallots.

4 Meanwhile, put the butter beans in a pan with the remaining garlic and cover with water. Bring to the boil and cook for 30 minutes until tender.

5 Place the pig meat in a large pan with the reserved cooking liquor, shallots and garlic. Add the cooked butter beans and bring to the boil. Gently simmer for 30 minutes.

6 Stir in the mustard to taste, season and simmer for 5 more minutes. Serve in small bowls and scatter with the parsley.

PALO CORTADO

TASTING NOTES Delicate and hazlenutty on the nose, rich and smooth to taste and beautiful bright mahogany in colour. **SERVING TEMPERATURE** Serve at room temperature. **FOOD** With nuts, fresh fruit, black pudding, smoked sausages, offal, red meat and game.

CHITTERLINGS WITH RADISHES

Best paired with:
AMONTILLADO,
OLOROSO

YOU MAY BE WARY OF THESE, BUT DO TRY THEM. THESE ARE THE PIG'S LOWER intestines, which have been brined and cooked. A dry amontillado holds its own against these chitterlings.

PREPARATION TIME: **15 MINUTES**   SERVES **4–6**

12 cm chitterlings | a generous handful breakfast radishes, leaves removed and reserved | 50 ml sherry vinegar | freshly ground black pepper, to season

1   Chop the chitterlings into small pieces and gently heat in a pan.

2   Add the breakfast radishes and season with black pepper. Splash with the sherry vinegar and warm everything through in the pan. Add the reserved radish leaves and stir until wilted. Serve.

SALT PORK & WALNUTS

Best paired with:
OLOROSO,
CREAM

MAKE SURE YOU PLAN AHEAD FOR WHEN YOU WANT THIS RECIPE. IT IS A GREAT ONE for Christmas time, so prepare in November for a delicious treat. The great thing with this recipe is that the quantities are up to you. Pork back fat and walnuts seem to speak the same language as 30-year-old oloroso.

PREPARATION TIME: **1 MONTH**

a piece of pork back fat | sea salt | walnuts in their shell

1 Put the pork back fat in a large dish and completely cover in sea salt. Chill in the fridge for a month.

2 After a month, brush off the salt and slice very thinly on to a plate.

3 Crack the walnuts open and extract the nuts. Break into pieces over the plated back fat. The best way to enjoy this dish, is to roll the pork back fat around a walnut to eat.

DEEP-FRIED WATERCRESS

Best paired with:
FINO

WHO WOULD HAVE THOUGHT TO DEEP-FRY THIS DELICATE LEAF BUT YOU WILL BE surprised how addictive it is to eat. This racy bushel of watercress is gently tamed by a crispy dry fino.

PREPARATION AND COOKING TIME: **10 MINUTES**   SERVES **6–8**

250 g cornflour | 250 ml cold water | 4 egg whites, lightly whisked | vegetable oil for deep-frying | 4 bunches watercress | salt, to season

1 In a bowl mix together with a wooden spoon the cornflour, cold water and egg whites to make a light batter.

2 Heat the vegetable oil in a deep-fat fryer or pan until a cube of bread browns in 30 seconds.

3 Then simply dip the bunches of watercress into the batter and carefully drop into the hot oil, in batches, for 30 seconds or until crisp. Remove and drain on kitchen paper. Season with salt and serve.

EWES' MILK CHEESE & PEA SALAD

Best paired with:
MANZANILLA,
FINO,
PALE CREAM

SALTY SHEEP'S CHEESE AND FRESH PEAS FROM THE POD IS UNIMAGINABLE WITHOUT A very well-chilled glass of manzanilla. If you can't get hold of fresh peas, then use defrosted frozen peas instead.

PREPARATION TIME: **15 MINUTES**   SERVES **4**

75 g fresh peas | 150 g wild rocket, roughly chopped | 75 g Berkswell sheep's milk cheese | 1 tablespoon red wine vinegar | squeeze of lemon juice | 4 tablespoons extra virgin olive oil | 2 tablespoons finely chopped fresh parley | 5 capers | salt and black pepper, to season

1 Put the peas and rocket in a bowl. Finely grate 50 g sheep's cheese and toss together.

2 In a jug, whisk together the red wine vinegar, lemon juice and extra virgin olive oil. Season to taste and then stir in the parsley and capers. Toss the dressing through the peas and rocket and divide amongst four plates.

3 Using a vegetable peeler cut slivers of the remaining cheese and use to top the salads. Serve immediately.

DUBLIN BORN, RICHARD CORRIGAN SHOWCASES HIS FOOD in classy surroundings: *Bentley's Oyster Bar and Grill,* restored to its former glory, an exclusive restaurant at the top of Norman Foster's 'gherkin', and the stylish, Michelin-starred *Lindsay House.*

With menus that often reflect his Celtic roots he admits he came to sherry late in life, but now he often enjoys a glass when eating out and is excited by the impact it has had on his cooking. His cooking creates menus of earthy and robust tastes and textures and sherry is a delightfully surprising match to some of these flavours: a nutty amontillado with the pepperiness of young turnips, for instance.

CURED PORK FILLET WITH APRICOTS, SAGE & TURNIPS

Best paired with:
AMONTILLADO,
PALO CORTADO

THIS IS A GREAT DISH BECAUSE IT CAN BE PREPARED IN ADVANCE. CAUL FAT IS THE LACY, fatty membrane encasing the internal organs of an animal. It comes in thin sheets and you can buy it from traditional butchers. If you want to make this and fresh apricots are out of season, use canned apricot halves in juice instead. This works perfectly with a nutty amontillado.

PREPARATION TIME: 20 MINUTES, PLUS CHILLING OVERNIGHT
COOKING TIME: 40 MINUTES   SERVES 4

2 pork fillets | small bunch of sage | 9 slices of Serrano ham | 250 g caul fat | 2 fresh apricots, quartered and stoned | 2 dessertspoons honey | 4 dessertspoons sherry vinegar | 1 tablespoon olive oil | 8 baby turnips, trimmed and halved | salt and black pepper, to season, to season

1 Wrap the pork with the sage leaves and then with the Serrano ham. Wrap with the caul fat, season and wrap tightly in cling film. Put into a shallow dish, cover completely with salt and chill overnight. Also put the apricots in a bowl with the honey and sherry vinegar and stir to coat. Chill overnight.

2 Preheat the oven to Gas Mark 7/220°C/450°F. Brush off the salt and remove the cling film from the pork. Heat the olive oil in a heavy-based pan and brown the pork fillets on all sides. Transfer to the oven and roast for 10 minutes and then leave to rest for 15 minutes.

3 Meanwhile, plunge the turnips in boiling, salted water and cook for a few minutes. Drain. Put the apricots in a pan with all the juices and the cooked turnips and gently heat to warm through.

4 Carve the pork and divide between four plates, add the turnips and apricots and spoon the apricot juices around the plate.

SAM & EDDIE HART

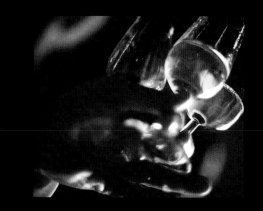

SAM HART STARTED HIS BUSINESS CAREER IN MEXICO CITY in 1996, where at the age of 22 he opened a cocktail bar. In June 2000 he went to live in Barcelona for six months, where he spent his days researching Spanish food. Leaving Barcelona thoroughly inspired, he returned to London to open the Spanish tapas restaurant *Fino* with his brother Eddie.

EDDIE, TOO, WAS DEEPLY INFLUENCED BY TIME IN SPAIN. He spent a year in Madrid, learning Spanish and developing a love for Spanish food and culture. Prior to creating *Fino*, he set up *Hart's Upstairs* at *Hart's* in Nottingham and also travelled to south east Australia to work in a winery. Their recipes offer the best in traditional tapas from the finest of British ingredients.

LAMB SWEETBREADS WITH PIQUILLO PEPPERS

THIS DISH WAS CREATED BY OUR HEAD CHEF JEAN PHILLIPE PATRUNO AND IS ALWAYS a hit at *Fino* when on the menu. Personally, we can eat this dish twice a day for a week! Try combining it with a glass of dry amontillado.

COOKING AND PREPARATION TIME: **20 MINUTES** SERVES **4–6**

1 tablespoon olive oil | 300 g lamb sweetbreads, outer skin removed | $^1/_2$ shallot, diced | 2 garlic cloves, chopped | 1 sprig of fresh thyme | 200 g piquillo peppers, thinly sliced lengthways | peel of $^1/_2$ lemon, finely sliced | 2 sprigs fresh oregano, chopped | salt and black pepper, to season, to season | chervil, to garnish

1 Heat the olive oil in a large frying pan over a high heat. Pan-fry the sweetbreads until golden brown all over.

2 Reduce the heat slightly and add the shallot and garlic to the pan, cook for 3 minutes. Add the thyme, peppers and lemon peel. Season with salt and black pepper and fry for a further 2–3 minutes. Stir through the oregano, garnish with chervil and serve immediately.

SPIDER CRAB WITH TOMATO & BASIL

Best paired with:
FINO

YOU RARELY SEE SPIDER CRABS ON ENGLISH MENUS YET THEY ARE TO BE FOUND IN abundance off the British coast. If you can't find spider crab try using the more common Cromer crab, that is just as delicious. Serve with lots of thinly sliced toast and a bottle of fino.

PREPARATION AND COOKING TIME: **30 MINUTES, PLUS COOLING**　SERVES **4**

2 kg live spider crab | 1 garlic clove, crushed | 2 basil leaves, shredded | 1 teaspoon wholegrain mustard | juice of $^1/_4$ lemon | $^1/_2$ small red chilli, de-seeded and diced | 4 tablespoons extra virgin olive oil | 6 small ripe tomatoes, peeled, seeded and diced | chervil, to garnish | salt and black pepper, to season

1　Heat a pan of heavily salted water until just boiling. Throw in the crab, bring back to the boil, reduce the heat to a vigorous simmer and cook for 10 minutes.

2　Remove the crab from the water and leave to cool for 30 minutes. Pick the meat from the crab, combining the white and dark meat in one bowl.

3　Add the garlic, basil, mustard, lemon juice, chilli, salt and pepper to taste and mix well. Whisk in the oil a little at a time until it has all been incorporated, then add the diced tomatoes. Garnish with some chervil and serve with thinly sliced toast.

FOIE GRAS WITH CHILLI JAM

Best paired with:
OLOROSO,
CREAM

WE HAVE SERVED THIS DISH AT *FINO* SINCE WE OPENED AND HAVE NO PLANS TO REMOVE it. We love the combination of the melt-in-the-mouth foie gras and the slightly sweet, spicy jam. Try drinking it with a cream sherry or a sweet oloroso.

PREPARATION TIME: **20 MINUTES** COOKING TIME: **45 MINUTES** SERVES **4**

6 red peppers, skinned, de-seeded and diced | 2 red chillies, finely chopped | 75 g caster sugar | 1 dessertspoon tomato purée | 6 tomatoes, skinned, de-seeded and diced | 2 dessertspoons cold water | 1 lobe foie gras extra, sliced into 1 cm thick rounds | salt and black pepper, to season | 4 red chillies, to garnish | sprigs of parsley, to garnish

1 To make the chilli jam sweat the red peppers, red chillies, caster sugar, tomato purée, tomatoes and cold water for 40 minutes in a large non-stick pan over a medium heat until the mixture is jammy. Season with salt and pepper to taste.

2 Heat a frying pan over a medium heat until almost smoking and pan-fry the foie gras for 1 minute each side. Allow to rest for a further minute then serve immediately with the jam. Garnish each plate with a chilli and a sprig of parsley.

CREAM

TASTING NOTES A very complex, rich nose with a palate of spices, candied fruit and toffee. **SERVING TEMPERATURE** Lightly chilled — excellent on the rocks with a slice of orange, or as a digestive at the end of a meal. **FOOD** A great tip is to try cream sherry with fresh brioche and foie gras or Roquefort cheese. Nuts, desserts such as crème brûlée or gingerbread and fresh fruit are also great partners.

COCKLES & CHILLIES

Best paired with:
MANZANILLA,
FINO

THE COCKLE IS OFTEN OVERLOOKED AS A SEAFOOD TREAT BUT IT CAN BE JUST AS GOOD, if not better than the clam. Here it is simply cooked in a light and spicy broth of sherry, garlic and chillies: serve with lots of bread to soak up the juices. Chilled manzanilla is the perfect accompaniment.

COOKING AND PREPARATION TIME: **15 MINUTES, PLUS 2 HOURS SOAKING**   SERVES **4**

1 tablespoon mild olive oil | 3 garlic cloves | 3 shallots, finely diced | 2 chillies, de-seeded and finely sliced | 500 g cockles | 250 ml manzanilla | a handful of flat leaf parsley, chopped | freshly ground black pepper, to season

1 Soak the cockles in salty water in a dark place for 2 hours to remove any grit or sand. Drain thoroughly.

2 Heat the olive oil in a large heavy-based pan until just beginning to smoke. Add the garlic, shallots and chillies and cook for 2 minutes.

3 Throw in the cockles and sherry and cook for 5 minutes until the cockles have opened (discard any that don't open). Season with black pepper, throw in the parsley and serve at once.

BABY SQUID WITH INKED WHITE BEANS

Best paired with:
MANZANILLA,
FINO

WE FIRST ATE THIS DELICIOUS TAPAS IN THE BOQUERIA MARKET IN BARCELONA, THE combination of pulses and seafood is typical of Catalan cooking. The robust flavours of this dish go perfectly with a glass or bottle of the older manzanilla pasada, which has a little more grip and structure than the younger manzanilla.

COOKING AND PREPARATION TIME: **25 MINUTES**   SERVES **4**

2 tablespoons mild olive oil | 350 g baby squid, cleaned | 1 onion, finely chopped | 2 bay leaves | 3 tomatoes, peeled, skinned and diced | 1 teaspoon squid ink | 160 g cooked white beans, such as cannellini beans | 200 ml good quality fish stock | a handful of flat leaf parsley, chopped | salt and black pepper, to season

1 Heat 1 tablespoon oil in a heavy-based frying pan until very hot. Throw in the squid and cook for 2 minutes. Empty the contents of the pan into a sieve, reserving the liquid and squid. Set aside.

2 In another heavy-based frying pan heat the remaining oil and gently fry the onion and bay leaves for 5 minutes until the onion becomes translucent. Add the diced tomatoes and cook for 2 minutes.

3 Add the reserved squid and cook for a further 2 minutes. Then add the squid ink and cook for 1 minute. Finally add the cooked beans, stock and reserved cooking liquid and simmer until reduced a little. Season with salt and pepper, throw in the parsley and serve at once with some good bread.

HESTON BLUMENTHAL'S
TOP SHERRY & FOOD PAIRINGS

HESTON BLUMENTHAL KNOWS THAT SHERRY'S UNIQUE VERSATILITY OFFERS A MYRIAD POTENTIAL PAIRINGS. Matching food and sherry has long been a passion and has led him to discover some of the most perfect combinations, where the pairing significantly intensifies the flavour and texture of the food whilst complementing the taste of the sherry.

MANZANILLA – SARDINES

The manzanilla cuts through the oiliness of the sardines, while the slightly yeasty and green apple notes of the sherry enhance the fresh aroma of the sardines. The slightly salty taste of the manzanilla is also enhanced by the umami taste of the sardines. Try tasting with thinly sliced Granny Smith apples.

FINO – WALNUTS

The tannic astringency of walnuts plays well with the dryness of fino sherry. The warm-spicy, sweet and rich tea leaf-like odour of the walnuts balances well with the balsamic and citrus overtones in the aroma of the sherry.

AMONTILLADO – PECORINO

The mild saltiness and umami taste of pecorino balances well with amontillado. Slight straw-like and citrus-like notes provide a nice complement to the aroma of this sherry. Try a drizzle of golden syrup over the cheese.

OLOROSO – FOIE GRAS

The acidity, and sweetness of the oloroso pairs very well with the texture of the foie gras. The slight dryness, toasted bread and roasted nut aromas of the sherry work really well with some fresh almonds and sour cherries.

PALO CORTADO – ROASTED HAZELNUTS

The complex fatty, nutty and roasted notes reinforce the fresh toasted bread and nutty notes in the palo cortado. Try coating the nuts in fine toasted and salted breadcrumbs.

PALE CREAM – MANGO

The soft, creamy and buttery flesh of the mango and an aroma reminiscent of peaches and coconut pair well with the almond and biscuit notes of the pale cream sherry. A few green peppercorns will make a wonderful contrast.

MEDIUM – CURRY LEAVES

The fresh and somewhat tangerine aroma of mild curry leaves can really enhance the caramel notes of this sherry.

CREAM – HOCK OF HAM

The salted pork flavour of the ham cuts through the richness of the cream sherry. In addition, the aromas of ripe apricot, peach, coconut and a very slight rose-like aroma of the ham are enhanced by the toffee and candied fruit aromas of this sherry.

MOSCATEL – RASPBERRIES

The very fresh, fruity, green and floral-like aroma of the raspberries pairs well with moscatel. In particular the slightly violet-like perfume with the seedy, woody background of the raspberries balances the caramel and balsamic notes of the sherry well.

PEDRO XIMÉNEZ – BITTER CHOCOLATE

The heavy, sweet, floral and spicy aromas of the chocolate are enhanced by the deep raisin, plum and black cherry notes in the PX.

VINEET BHATIA

BORN IN INDIA IN 1967, VINEET BHATIA DEVELOPED HIS passion for food from his mother. Many of my influences in the creation of my recipes come from my mother. She had a fantastic imagination when it came to cooking and I have yet to taste food quite like it.

After studying and working in Bombay, Vineet arrived in London in 1993 and was immediately disappointed with the representation of Indian food in the country at that time. In 2004 Vineet realised his long-cherished dream when he opened *Rasoi* (kitchen) with life partner Rashima. The hard work finally paid off in January 2006 when *Rasoi* was awarded the coveted Michelin star.

Vineet draws on the eclectic mix of Indian cooking that surrounded him in Bombay to create grazing dishes that combine traditional and modern and for this, sherry is the matching wine of choice. A cream sherry is the perfect foil for a spicy curry and matches the sweetness of an accompanying chutney.

MASALA CRAB CAKES WITH CRAB MAYONNAISE

Best paired with:
AMONTILLADO,
PALO CORTADO,
PALE CREAM

THIS IS A DISH INSPIRED FROM MY CHILDHOOD FAVOURITE TEATIME SNACK OF 'POTATO tikki'. Here I have incorporated crab along with the potatoes to give it a twist. Accompany with a light, pale cream sherry that supports the delicateness of the crabmeat and has a sweetness that lifts the flavours of the dish. The acidity of the wine balances the crab cake.

PREPARATION AND COOKING TIME: **40 MINUTES**   SERVES **4**

FOR THE CRAB CAKES: $2^1/_2$ tablespoons vegetable oil | $1^1/_2$ teaspoons mustard seeds | 10 curry leaves, coarsely chopped | 1 small onion, finely chopped | $1^1/_2$ teaspoons chopped garlic | $1^1/_2$ teaspoons chopped ginger | $1^1/_2$ teaspoons chopped green chilli | 1 teaspoon red chilli powder | 1 teaspoon turmeric | 65 g brown crabmeat | 100 g cooked potatoes, grated | salt, to taste | 1 teaspoon chaat masala (available from good Indian supermarkets) | 65 g white crabmeat | 3 eggs | 200 g fresh breadcrumbs | vegetable oil for deep-frying | **FOR THE CRAB MAYONNAISE:** 75 g white crabmeat| 1 large spring onion, finely chopped| $^1/_2$ large tomato, de-seeded and finely diced | $1^1/_2$ tablespoons vegetable oil | 1 teaspoon mustard seeds | 5 curry leaves, chopped | 3 tablespoons good quality mayonnaise | squeeze of lemon juice | cress, Japanese sakura (cherry) leaves and diced tomatoes, to garnish

1 Heat the oil in a large pan and add the mustard seeds. As they begin to crackle, add the curry leaves and chopped onion and cook for 3–4 minutes. Then add the chopped garlic, ginger and green chilli and cook for a few more minutes.

2 Mix the red chilli powder and turmeric powder with 1 tablespoon water. Add to the pan and cook for a minute. Add the brown crabmeat and fry until all the moisture has evaporated. Then stir in the grated potatoes and season with salt and chaat masala.

3 Stir in the white crabmeat and remove from the heat. Beat together 2 eggs and stir into the mixture. Using wet hands shape the crab mixture into round patties and chill until needed.

4 Meanwhile, make the mayonnaise. Mix the white crabmeat with the spring onion and tomato. Heat the oil in a pan and add the mustard seeds and curry leaves. When the seeds begin to crackle, take the pan off the heat and stir into the crab mixture. Mix in the mayonnaise and lemon juice and season. Chill until needed.

5 Whisk the remaining egg in a bowl and dip the crab patties into the beaten egg and then the breadcrumbs in batches.

6 Heat the vegetable oil in a pan until a cube of bread browns in 60 seconds. Carefully deep-fry the crab cakes, in batches, until golden and heated through. Drain on kitchen paper and serve with the crab mayonnaise.

TANDOORI LOBSTER WITH SAFFRON UPMA & LOBSTER CHILLI OIL

Best paired with:
FINO, YOUNG
PALO CORTADO

THIS DISH MARRIES A VERY HUMBLE, TRADITIONAL SOUTH INDIAN BREAKFAST DISH, upma, with luxurious lobster, cooked with a classic technique resulting in outstanding complementary flavours. A dry style of fino sherry works very well with the flavour of the lobster, without overpowering it, and also copes with the saffron in the dish. The lobster oil will last for 2 weeks.

PREPARATION AND COOKING TIME: **1 HOUR, PLUS 6½ HOURS MARINATING**   SERVES **4**

FOR THE TANDOORI LOBSTER: 1 tablespoon ginger purée | 1 tablespoon garlic purée | 1 tablespoon lemon juice | a little salt | 4 x 100 g lobster tails | 4 tablespoons thick natural yoghurt | 1 teaspoon turmeric | 1 teaspoon red chilli powder | 1 teaspoon carom seeds or ajwan seeds | 1 teaspoon garam masala | 2 tablespoons vegetable oil | **FOR THE LOBSTER CHILLI OIL:** 200 ml olive oil | 500 g lobster shells, coarsely crushed | 3 garlic cloves, coarsely chopped | 2 red chillies, coarsely chopped | 3 tablespoons tomato purée | **FOR THE SAFFRON UPMA:** 4 tablespoons vegetable oil | 1½ teaspoons mustard seeds | 1 tablespoon finely chopped ginger | 1 tablespoon finely chopped green chilli | 8 curry leaves, coarsely chopped | 75 g coarse semolina | a generous pinch of saffron strands, soaked in 150 ml hot water | 150 ml coconut milk | 1 tablespoon lemon juice | 1 tablespoon caster sugar | 25 g butter | 50 g whole blanched almonds, toasted | salt, to season

1   Mix together the ginger and garlic purées, lemon juice and a little salt in a bowl. Add the lobster tails and stir to coat in the marinade. Set aside for 30 minutes.

2   In another bowl mix together the yoghurt, turmeric, chilli powder, carom seeds, garam masala and vegetable oil. Put the marinated lobster into this new marinade and chill in the fridge for 6 hours.

3   Meanwhile, make the lobster oil. Heat the oil in a deep pan with the chopped lobster shells and cook until the shells begin to discolour and turn pink.

4   Add the garlic, red chilli and tomato purée and cook on a low heat for 20 minutes. Remove from the heat and allow to cool. Pass through a sieve and preserve in a sterilised bottle.

5   Preheat the oven to Gas Mark 6/200°C/400°F. To make the upma, heat the oil in a deep pan and add the mustard seeds. As they begin to crackle add the ginger and chilli and cook for 30 seconds.

6   Add the curry leaves and semolina, stirring until the semolina releases a nutty aroma. Then stir in the saffron and water, coconut milk, lemon juice, sugar and salt to taste.

7   Bring to the boil, reduce the heat and simmer until the semolina is cooked and the water has dried out. Stir in the butter and keep warm.

8   Remove the lobster from the marinade and sear in a hot pan to seal on all sides. Transfer to the oven for 7–8 minutes until cooked. To assemble, spoon a quenelle of semolina on a plate, sprinkle around almonds and a generous drizzle of the lobster oil. Top with the lobster tails and serve.

ROASTED DUCK SEEKH KEBAB WITH PINEAPPLE CHUTNEY

Best paired with:
MEDIUM,
CREAM,
MOSCATEL

SEEKH KEBAB IS A NORTH INDIAN DISH CLASSICALLY INCORPORATING LAMB. HERE I HAVE USED duck meat balancing it with the pineapple chutney. The sweetness of cream sherry matches the sweetness of the pineapple chutney. The richer, nuttier style of the wine enables it to cope with the spices and harmonises with the duck kebab.

PREPARATION AND COOKING TIME: 1 HOUR 25 MINUTES, PLUS 3 HOURS MARINATING
SERVES 4

FOR THE DUCK SEEKH KEBAB: 200 g boneless and skinless duck thighs, cut into 4 cm cubes | 1¹/₂ tablespoons chopped garlic | 1¹/₂ tablespoons chopped ginger | 2 tablespoons chopped fresh coriander | 1 tablespoon chopped fresh mint | 1 tablespoon chopped green chilli | 1 teaspoon garam masala | salt, to season | FOR THE PINEAPPLE CHUTNEY: 2 teaspoons vegetable oil | 1 teaspoon fennel seeds, lightly crushed | 1 teaspoon chopped garlic | 1 teaspoon chopped ginger | ¹/₂ medium golden pineapple, peeled, cored and finely chopped | 1 tablespoon white wine vinegar | 1 teaspoon black peppercorns, lightly crushed | 1¹/₂ tablespoons caster sugar | ¹/₂ teaspoon ground green cardamom | onion seed sprouts, to garnish

1 Put all the ingredients for the duck seekh kebab into a bowl and season with salt. Stir well to coat and chill in the fridge for 2 hours.

2 Pass the marinated duck ingredients through a fine mincer or whiz in a food processor until minced. Transfer the mixture to a bowl and knead together with your hands. Chill in the fridge for 1 hour. This helps the mixture to bind well and makes it easier to skewer.

3 Meanwhile, make the pineapple chutney. Heat the oil in a deep pan, add the fennel seeds and, as they begin to discolour, add the garlic and ginger. Cook for 1 minute.

4 Add the pineapple and bring to the boil. Reduce the heat, cover and simmer for 30 minutes or until the pineapple softens and turns into a liquid state.

5 Add the white wine vinegar, black peppercorns and sugar. Cook for a further 5 minutes and add the ground cardamom.

6 Bring the mixture to a boil, remove from the heat and allow to go cold. Preheat the oven to Gas Mark 7/220°C/450°F.

7 Shape the duck mince around skewers and roast in the oven for 6–10 minutes until cooked. Once cooked, remove from the skewer and slice. Serve with the pineapple chutney, scattered with onion sprouts.

MALAI CHICKEN TIKKA WITH COCONUT KHICHDI

Best paired with:
OLOROSO,
CREAM

KHICHDI CAN BE BEST DESCRIBED AS AN INDIAN STYLE RISOTTO, PERHAPS OF A THINNER consistency. The khichdi I do bears no resemblance to the traditional one – it is richer, uses different ingredients than the classically used lentils and has more body and character. Try a dry oloroso, a complex sherry that reflects the flavours of the coconut and pine kernels in the dish. The oloroso easily holds up to the cheese marinade and the creaminess of the chicken tikka. For a special touch drizzle chilli chutney on the plate by whizzing up red chillies, garlic, yoghurt and oil until puréed.

PREPARATION TIME: **15 MINUTES, PLUS 8**$\frac{1}{2}$ **HOURS MARINATING**
COOKING TIME: **25 MINUTES**   SERVES **4**

FOR THE MALAI CHICKEN: 4 skinless chicken breasts, cut into 4 cm cubes | 1 tablespoon ginger purée | 1 tablespoon garlic purée | 1 tablespoon lemon juice | 4 tablespoons grated Cheddar | 2 tablespoons grated mozzarella | 3 tablespoons natural yoghurt | 3 tablespoons single cream | 1 tablespoon chopped ginger | 1$\frac{1}{2}$ teaspoons chopped green chilli | 2 tablespoons chopped fresh coriander | 1 teaspoon freshly ground black pepper | $\frac{1}{3}$ teaspoon ground green cardamom | salt | **FOR THE COCONUT KHICHDI:** 2 tablespoons olive oil | 25 g butter | 2 shallots, sliced | 1 teaspoon chopped ginger | 1 teaspoon chopped green chillies | 150 g basmati rice | 300 ml chicken stock | 125 ml coconut milk | 25 g grated coconut, plus shavings to garnish | 2 tablespoons toasted pine kernels

1 For the malai chicken mix the chicken in a bowl with the ginger and garlic purées and lemon juice. Chill for 30 minutes.

2 Mix all the remaining ingredients for the chicken in a bowl to make a smooth paste. Then coat the chicken with this mixture and chill for 8 hours.

3 Make the coconut khichdi just before serving: heat the oil and butter in a large pan and cook the shallots for 3–4 minutes until translucent. Stir in the ginger and green chillies and cook for a further 2 minutes.

4 Stir in the basmati rice, then add the stock and bring it to boil. Reduce the heat and simmer for 5 minutes. Meanwhile, preheat the grill to hot and thread the chicken on to skewers.

5 Pour the coconut milk into the rice and cook for a further 10 minutes until the rice is tender. Stir in the grated coconut, pine kernels and season to taste. Meanwhile, place the chicken skewers under the grill and cook for 10 minutes, turning until cooked. Serve the skewers with the rice garnished with coconut shavings.

CARDAMOM RICE PUDDING WITH HONEY & CUMIN GLAZED FIGS

Best paired with:
CREAM,
PEDRO XIMÉNEZ

RICE PUDDING IS ONE OF THE MOST UNIVERSALLY RECOGNISED DESSERTS, EATEN IN different countries by many different religions. Indian rice pudding incorporates the use of spices such as cardamom and cinnamon and different nuts. Here I have used fresh figs with a touch of cumin, adding more soul to the pudding. Personally, I like to have the rice pudding cold with warm caramelised figs. For a quick caramel see page 128. A rich and sweet Pedro Ximénez stands up well, both to the spice as well as to the sweetness of the rice pudding. It mirrors the consistency of the pudding and you can taste wine flavours similar to the dried figs incorporated in the dish.

PREPARATION TIME: **40 MINUTES**   COOKING TIME: **20 MINUTES**   SERVES **4**

FOR THE HONEY AND CUMIN GLAZED FIGS: 40 g unsalted butter, softened | 6 tablespoons runny honey | 1 teaspoon grated lemon zest | 2 teaspoons lemon juice | 1 tablespoon cumin seeds, roasted | 1/2 teaspoon green cardamom powder | 8 figs, halved | **FOR THE CARDAMOM RICE PUDDING:** 125 g basmati rice, coarsely crushed and rinsed | 400 ml full fat milk | 125 g granulated sugar | 1/2 teaspoon ground green cardamom

1 In a bowl mix together all the ingredients for the honey and cumin glazed figs, except the figs. Then gently stir in the figs to coat and set aside for 30 minutes. At the same time soak the rice in warm water for 30 minutes and drain. This helps remove the starch.

2 Preheat the oven to Gas Mark 4/180°C/375°F. Put the rice and milk into a heavy-based pan and bring to the boil. Reduce the heat and simmer for about 20 minutes, stirring occasionally until the rice is completely cooked and the milk nearly all absorbed. It should be quite thick in consistency.

3 Stir in the sugar, remove from the heat, stir in the ground cardamom and cover.

4 Place the figs on a roasting tray and cook in the oven for 5 minutes until tender and sticky. Serve with cardamom rice pudding.

PEDRO XIMÉNEZ (PX)

TASTING NOTES The darkest of the sherries with deep mahogany colouring. Pick up caramel and raisins on the nose. Full-bodied and luxurious, with flavours of chocolate and caramel. **SERVING TEMPERATURE** Room temperature. **FOOD** Ice cream with Pedro Ximénez drizzled over the top. Just delicious! Or for something more indulgent add pancakes and chocolate sauce. Also rich foods such as blue cheese or chocolate, and superb with Christmas pudding.

MARCUS WAREING,
CHEF-PATRON *PÉTRUS*, THE BERKELEY, LONDON

MARCUS IS A RELATIVELY NEW CONVERT TO THE PLEASURES of sherry. He acknowledges that sherry, being so powerful in its own right, can take on a lot of powerful flavours. Sweet can balance salty as well as strong, dry sherries being able to hold their own with robust, spicy flavours.

"The flavour is amazingly diverse."

Marcus' restaurant career started at *The Savoy* when he was just eighteen, since then he has worked alongside luminaries such as Albert Roux and Gordon Ramsay. In 2003 *Pétrus* was awarded the AA's ultimate accolade of five rosettes and Marcus was voted the Cateys (Caterer and Hotelkeeper Awards) 'Chef of the Year'.

BABY ARTICHOKES À LA GRECQUE WITH FIGS & PARMA HAM

Best paired with:
AMONTILLADO,
OLOROSO

A FRAGRANT OLOROSO PROVIDES THE PERFECT FOIL FOR THIS DISH, CUTTING THROUGH the rich flavour. To make stock syrup put 100 g granulated sugar in a pan and pour over 200 ml warm water. Brush the sides of the pan with water to rinse away any sugar. Gently heat until the sugar has dissolved and then boil for 2 minutes. Allow to cool and then use. To prepare the artichokes squeeze the juice of one lemon into a large bowl of water. Cut the stems off the artichokes leaving about 4 cm remaining. Remove two or three rows of leaves from the base, peel the artichoke bases and stems and cut 1 cm from the top of the leaves. Place the artichokes in the bowl of lemon water until needed.

PREPARATION TIME: **20 MINUTES** COOKING TIME: **40 MINUTES**   SERVES **4**

1 litre water | 250 ml olive oil | 350 ml white wine vinegar | 5 coriander seeds, crushed | 2 shallots, chopped | 5 white peppercorns, crushed | 4 baby artichokes | 200 ml stock syrup | 300 ml red wine | 1 star anise | 1 cinnamon stick | 4 ripe figs | 4 black stoned olives, quartered | 4 basil leaves, chopped, plus extra to garnish | 4 slices good quality Parma ham

1 Put the water, olive oil, 250 ml white wine vinegar, coriander seeds, shallots and peppercorns in a pan and bring to the boil. Pass through a sieve and then return to a clean pan.

2 Add the artichokes to the pan and bring to the boil. Simmer for 15 minutes or until the artichokes are cooked. Leave them to cool in the cooking liquor.

3 Put the stock syrup, remaining white wine vinegar, red wine, star anise and cinnamon in a pan and bring to the boil. Put the figs in a bowl and pour the hot liquid over the figs. Leave them to go cold.

4 Remove the figs, cut into small cubes and put into a bowl. Set aside. Pass the fig cooking liquid through a sieve and return to a pan. Bring to the boil and cook until syrupy.

5 Mix the olives, basil and 1 tablespoon of the syrup into the figs. Remove the artichokes from the cooking liquor. With a small spoon scoop out the middle of the choke leaving a little hole.

6 Spoon a little of the fig mixture into the hole to fill the artichokes. Gently heat a non-stick pan and lightly colour the artichokes. Drain on kitchen paper.

7 Cut the artichokes in half and arrange on the plates with crumpled Parma ham, drizzle with a little of the fig syrup and garnish with basil leaves.

JASON ATHERTON

JASON ATHERTON WAS THE FIRST BRITISH CHEF TO complete a stage at Spain's famous *El Bulli* restaurant, working for the renowned chef Ferrán Adrià. Since then Jason has been a trendsetter, introducing tapas-style eating to the UK and offering a wide variety of tasting dishes at the Michelin-starred restaurant *maze*.

"The list of sherries at *El Bulli* is second to none, and this is where I learned the respect that this great product deserves."

Jason has worked under Pierre Koffman, Nico Ladenis and Gordon Ramsay as executive chef at *Verre* in Dubai. He is now head chef at *maze*, the latest addition to the Gordon Ramsay Group.

ORKNEY SCALLOPS WITH PEPPERED GOLDEN RAISIN & CAULIFLOWER PURÉE

Best paired with:
FINO,
AMONTILLADO

SERVE CHILLED, FRUITY AND LIGHT FINO TO CUT THROUGH THE SWEETNESS OF THE purées. For the mixed peppercorns try pink, white, Sarawak and micro green peppercorns for a spicy mix.

PREPARATION AND COOKING TIME: **40 MINUTES, PLUS 2 HOURS RESTING**   SERVES **4**

1 large head cauliflower, cut into small florets | 300 ml full fat milk | 300 ml single cream | 500 g golden raisins | 500 g king scallops, halved | a little mild curry powder | salt | 4 tablespoons mixed peppercorns, ground to a powder | micro-greens, to garnish

1 Put the cauliflower in a pan with the milk and cream and simmer for 20–30 minutes until really soft. Whiz in a blender until smooth and season with salt and the pepper mix. Keep warm.

2 Meanwhile put the raisins in a pan with enough water to cover. Bring to the boil and simmer until they are soft and plump. Allow to cool slightly, then whiz in a blender until smooth. Season with salt and the pepper mix. Keep warm.

3 Dust the scallops with mild curry powder and salt. Pan-fry in a very hot pan for 30 seconds on each side.

4 To serve, arrange the scallops on top of the cauliflower purée and add the raisin purée to the plate. Garnish with micro-greens.

FINO

TASTING NOTES Pale, lemon tinged with a fresh almondy nose. **SERVING TEMPERATURE** Well chilled, so stick it in the fridge for a couple of hours before pouring. Fino is also meant to be drunk like a chardonnay, so there's no need to hold back with the measures. **FOOD** Always recommended with Serrano ham, Spanish olives and soups. However fino's light character makes it a great all-rounder going well with tapas, cheeses, almonds, artichokes, asparagus, salami and all types of fish – including sushi.

ROASTED FOIE GRAS WITH SMOKED HALIBUT & CHOUCROUTE

Best paired with: AMONTILLADO, MEDIUM, CREAM

WAKE UP YOUR TASTE BUDS WITH THIS RICH DISH JUST BURSTING WITH FLAVOURS. The soft and nutty amontillado has a touch of caramel and smoky raisin flavours that complement the luxurious foie gras amazingly. Garnish with celery shoots for a little freshness.

PREPARATION AND COOKING TIME: **45 MINUTES**   SERVES **4**

4 x 100g foie gras | 25 g butter | 200 g smoked halibut, thinly sliced | FOR THE MANZANILLA SAUCE: 25 g butter | 5 shallots, finely chopped | $\frac{1}{2}$ head of garlic, cut horizontally | 8 sprigs of thyme | 3 bay leaves | 250 ml manzanilla sherry | 500 ml chicken stock | 500 ml veal stock | FOR THE ONION VELOUTÉ: 125 g butter | 4 white onions, thinly sliced | 250 ml single cream | FOR THE CHOUCROUTE: 6 juniper berries | 1 smoked streaky bacon rasher, chopped | 25 g butter | $\frac{1}{2}$ white cabbage, outer leaves removed, cored and finely shredded | 100 ml white wine | 100 ml white wine vinegar | salt and black pepper, to season

1 To make the manzanilla sauce, melt the butter in a pan and cook the shallots and garlic for 5 minutes. Add the thyme and bay leaves and continue to cook until the shallots start to caramelise.

2 Pour in the sherry and rapidly boil to deglaze the pan. Add both the stocks, bring to the boil and simmer for 20 minutes.

3 Meanwhile make the onion velouté. Melt the butter in a large pan and gently cook the onions for 3–4 minutes until softened. Strain off the butter and then whiz the onions with a hand blender.

4 Pass through a fine sieve, then return to a clean pan with the cream and rapidly boil until thick. Whiz again with a hand blender and pass through a sieve. Season to taste and keep warm.

5 Strain the manzanilla sauce through a fine sieve and return to a clean pan. Bring to the boil and simmer until reduced by three quarters, skimming the surface constantly. Keep warm and set aside.

6 For the choucroute wrap the juniper berries and bacon in muslin. Melt the butter in a large pan and cook the shredded cabbage with the bacon muslin for 5–10 minutes until nearly tender.

7 Add the white wine and the white wine vinegar and bring to the boil. Simmer until the juices have been absorbed. Season.

8 To serve, pan-fry the foie gras in the butter for a few minutes. Divide the slices of smoked halibut between 4 plates and top with a small spoonful of the choucroute. Top with the foie gras and drizzle around the manzanilla sauce. Whiz the velouté to make it light and foamy and spoon on top of the foie gras. Serve immediately.

ROAST PIGEON WITH SPRING CABBAGE PURÉE & VANILLA SHALLOTS

Best paired with:
OLOROSO,
CREAM

OLOROSO, BURSTING WITH SMOKY WOOD AND PRUNE FLAVOURS, PERFECTLY COMPLEMENTS the fruity, gamey and sweet flavours in this impressive take on a traditional dish.

PREPARATION AND COOKING TIME: **1 HOUR**   SERVES **4**

2 tablespoons olive oil | 2 garlic cloves | 4 pigeon legs | 3 shallots | 1 bay leaf | 1 carrot, peeled and diced | 1 celery stick, diced | a few sprigs of thyme | 4 tablespoons sherry vinegar | 175 ml white wine | 175 ml Madeira | 750 ml white chicken stock | 750 ml veal stock | 4 pigeon crowns | salt and black pepper, to season, to season | **FOR THE DATE AND BACON SANDWICH:** 8 thin slices pancetta | 2 banana shallots, finely chopped | a large sprig of thyme | 25 g butter | 250 g ready to eat dates, stoned | 150 ml chicken stock | **FOR THE VANILLA SHALLOTS AND SPRING CABBAGE PURÉE:** 2 tablespoons olive oil | 10 shallots, finely sliced | 1 vanilla pod, split in half and seeds scraped out and reserved | 250 ml chicken stock | 75 ml double cream | 1 head of spring cabbage, outer leaves removed, cored and finely shredded | salt and black pepper, to season

1 Heat the olive oil in a large pan and fry the garlic, pigeon legs, shallots, bay leaf, vegetables and thyme for a few minutes until golden brown. Season.

2 Preheat the oven to Gas Mark 2/150˚C/300˚F. Add the sherry vinegar and bubble for a few minutes to deglaze the pan. Pour in the wine and Madeira and simmer until it is sticky and reduced. Pour in both stocks and gently simmer for 20 minutes. Keep warm.

3 For the date and bacon sandwich, bake the pancetta between 2 baking trays for 20 minutes in the oven until golden and crisp. Allow to cool.

4 For the vanilla shallots, heat the olive oil in a pan and gently cook the shallots for 10 minutes until caramelised. Add the vanilla seeds and season. Keep warm.

5 For the cabbage purée, pour the chicken stock into a pan and bring to the boil. Simmer until reduced by half to about 125 ml. Set aside. In another pan, bring the cream to the boil and simmer until reduced by half. Set aside.

6 Meanwhile, plunge the shredded cabbage into a large pan of boiling water and cook for 5 minutes until tender. Drain and allow to cool slightly.

7 Whiz the cabbage in a blender, adding the reduced stock and cream a little at a time until it is smooth. Pass the purée through a fine sieve and season. Keep warm.

8 Increase the oven to Gas Mark6/200˚C/ 400˚F. For the date and bacon sandwich gently fry the shallots and thyme in the butter until soft. Add the dates and chicken stock and simmer until the dates are soft. Whiz in a food processor until puréed. Set aside.

9 Roast the pigeons on the crown in the oven for 5–6 minutes until they are golden brown and pink in the centre.

10 Allow the meat to rest for 2 minutes then take the breasts off the bone. Pipe the prune purée between 2 slices of pancetta to make a sandwich. Repeat to make 3 more. Divide the cabbage purée between the plates and top with a spoonful of vanilla shallots. Place the breast and a leg on the top of the shallots. Rest the date and bacon sandwich on top and drizzle the sauce from the pigeon legs around.

CHOCOLATE SORBET FONDANT

Best paired with:
CREAM,
MOSCATEL,
PEDRO XIMÉNEZ

THE SOFT AND MELLOW FLAVOURS OF CARAMEL AND HONEY FROM PEDRO XIMÉNEZ are fantastic with these little chocolate puddings. This is delicious served with vanilla and pecan ice cream.

PREPARATION TIME: **1 HOUR, PLUS CHILLING AND FREEZING**   SERVES **6**

400 g dark chocolate | 200 g caster sugar | 200 ml cold water | 8 egg yolks | 700 ml double cream | 100 ml full fat milk | **FOR THE BASE:** 150 g white chocolate | 188 g jar praline paste | 75 g cocoa butter | 250 g paillette feullitage or butter | **FOR THE CHOCOLATE SORBET:** 1 litre full fat milk | 500 g double cream | 375 g trimoline or liquid glucose | 250 g dark chocolate, melted | 175 g cocoa powder

1 For the base, melt the white chocolate, praline paste and cocoa butter in a bowl over a pan of barely simmering water. When the mix is smooth add the feullitage and stir until evenly combined.

2 Roll out the mix between 2 sheets of greaseproof paper until about 5 mm thick. Transfer to a baking tray and chill until set. Once set, cut out 6 circles to cover the base of 4 cm ring moulds. Chill until needed.

3 To make the sorbet put the milk, cream and trimoline together in a pan and bring to the boil. Stir in the melted chocolate and the cocoa powder and bring to the boil.

4 Pass through a fine sieve and transfer to an ice cream maker and, following the manufacturer's instructions, churn until frozen.

5 Make balls of frozen sorbet using an ice cream scoop and freeze on a baking tray lined with baking parchment. The sorbet balls will need to fit in the centre of each ring mould, leaving a 1 cm edge.

6 Melt the dark chocolate in a bowl over a pan of simmering water. Set aside. Put the sugar and water in a pan and bring to the boil until it reaches 120°C.

7 Whisk the egg yolks until foamy then pour over the sugar syrup, whisking until cold. Whisk the cream and milk until a very light ribbon stage. Add the egg yolk mixture to the warm chocolate. Fold in half the cream until evenly combined, then gently fold in the rest. Pour some of the chocolate filling half way up each ring mould. Then place a frozen chocolate sorbet ball in the centre of each. Pour over the remaining chocolate filling, level off and chill until to set.

8 To serve, carefully warm the ring moulds in hot water and remove the fondant.

"Since my time at *El Bulli* I have always used sherry in my cooking and featured it on my wine list. Now at *maze* I have a whole page dedicated to it. Sherry is also largely used in our tasting menus for which we have become so well known. Laura, my sommelier, and I have worked hard on the food and wine pairing at *maze*."

PETER GORDON

NEW ZEALAND-BORN PETER GORDON, WHOSE FOOD STYLE, loosely called 'fusion', was initially inspired by a year of travel throughout South East Asia, considers 'the world's culinary resources as one huge, exciting larder'. It is not surprising therefore that he is a huge fan of matching sherry to food. 'From the dry flinty finos through to the exploding sweet fruit on the tongue of PX and muscatels, sherry has a character to go with almost any flavour.'

"The most surprising thing about sherry is that most people are unaware of its delicious range of flavours and textures. Sherry imparts a certain purity that few other wines do. A clean palate that rolls out of the glass complementing the food you have with it."

Peter spent five years living and cooking in Australia before returning to New Zealand to set up *The Sugar Club* in Wellington. Peter moved to London in 1989 and is the author of four best-selling cookbooks as well as having become a well-known TV personality; in 2001 he and Anna Hanson opened *The Providores*.

SLOW COOKED LAMB WITH POMEGRANATE ROASTED GRAPE SALAD

Best paired with:
DRY OLOROSO,
PALO CORTADO

THIS SALAD IS QUITE A QUIRKY MIXTURE OF FLAVOURS AND TEXTURES BUT ONE THAT works really well. Serve it warm for the most flavour. One lamb shoulder will give you a lot of meat, probably enough for 15 or so tapas style dishes, but here I give quantities for just 6 portions in total. The lamb meat will keep in the fridge, covered tightly, for up to 5 days. Pomegranate molasses is a sour yet sweet syrup and gives a rich fruit flavour to the grapes; you can buy it online. A rich, nutty palo cortado goes really well with the lamb as it carries the flavoursome fat of the meat along your tongue and gives both itself and the meat length of flavour.

PREPARATION TIME: **25 MINUTES** COOKING TIME: **3 HOURS**   SERVES **6**

$2^1/_2$ teaspoons sweet smoked paprika | 2 teaspoons coarse sea salt | 1 small New Zealand lamb shoulder | a small handful of mint sprigs | a small handful of fresh thyme sprigs | 150 ml boiling water | 200 g seedless red grapes | 2 tablespoons pomegranate molasses | 3 tablespoons extra virgin Spanish olive oil | 6 tablespoons Greek yoghurt | 24 walnut halves, toasted | the seeds from $^1/_2$ a pomegranate

1 Preheat the oven to Gas Mark 4/180°C/350°F. Rub 2 teaspoons of the paprika and the coarse sea salt over the lamb and place in a large roasting pan.

2 Remove the mint leaves from the stalks and reserve. Place the stalks along with the thyme in with the lamb and pour on the boiling water.

3 Place a sheet of baking parchment loosely on the lamb, then seal tightly with foil and bake for $2^1/_2$–3 hours.

4 After 2 hours, place the grapes, the remaining paprika, pomegranate molasses and olive oil in an ovenproof dish. Cook in the oven with the lamb for about 30 minutes or until the grape skins begin to wrinkle.

5 Remove the grapes from the oven and leave to cool. Coarsely shred the mint leaves and stir into the roasted grapes. The lamb is ready when it begins to shrink from the bone. To check, fold back a corner of the foil and paper from the roasting dish and test it with a knife – it should be soft and tender.

6 Once the lamb is ready remove the foil and paper and leave it to cool a little. Remove the flesh from the bones and either tear or cut it into chunks, discarding excess fat, and keep warm. Reserve the cooking juices and keep warm.

7 To serve, place about 75 g lamb meat on each plate in a slight mound. Spoon the roasted grapes and their juices over the lamb. Place a dollop of yoghurt on each plate, scatter with the walnuts and pomegranate seeds and drizzle with the reserved lamb juices.

SCALLOP & TURBOT YUZU SALAD WITH WATERMELON

Best paired with:
FINO,
PALE CREAM

FOR THIS DISH TO WORK ITS MAGIC EVERYTHING HAS TO BE PERFECT. THE TURBOT AND scallops need to be in prime form and the watermelon needs to be sweet and juicy but firm. Yuzu is a citrus fruit grown commercially in Japan and is reminiscent of a mixture of grapefruit and tangerine. It generally comes salted and juiced from Japanese supermarkets. You can use lime juice mixed with a dash of mirin instead. Micro-greens are basically the shoots before the vegetable or salad leaves have grown. Try broccoli shoots, pea shoots, fennel shoots for an intense, fresh flavour. The flinty fresh biscuity notes of pale cream give an applauding hand to raw fish and fresh fruit. The crisp cold sweet watermelon, combined with the raw fish and citrus fruit yuzu, plays wonderfully on the tongue.

PREPARATION: **20 MINUTES**   SERVES **4**

4 large scallops with coral, cleaned | 1 teaspoon yuzu juice | 125 g turbot fillet, skin and bones removed | 2 teaspoons light soy sauce | 200 g watermelon, skin and seeds removed | 1 tablespoon extra virgin **Spanish** olive oil | wood sorrel or other micro-greens, to garnish

1 Put 4 plates in the fridge to chill. Remove the coral from the scallops and finely chop – you'll need just 1 tablespoon; discard the rest. Mix in 2 drops of the yuzu juice and chill in the fridge until needed.

2 Slice each scallop into 3 discs and brush with the remaining yuzu. Slice the turbot into 3 mm slices, brush with the soy sauce and chill both in the fridge until needed.

3 Cut the watermelon into 8 even sized slices and put 1 slice on each chilled plate. Top the watermelon with a little sliced turbot, then with another slice of watermelon. Finish each plate with 3 scallop slices and a small amount of the chopped coral. Drizzle with the olive oil and scatter with the wood sorrel.

"The flinty fresh biscuity notes of pale cream give an applauding hand to raw fish and fresh fruit. The crisp cold sweet watermelon, combined with the raw fish and citrus fruit yuzu, plays wonderfully on the tongue."

GARLICKY SNAILS ON CHORIZO MASH

CHORIZO IS A LIGHTLY CURED SPANISH SAUSAGE AND COMES IN A VARIETY OF FORMS. For this dish you need to use cooking chorizo (chorizo *perilla*) and then all that's left to do is decide if you want to have it spicy (chorizo *picante*) or mild. The intense chorizo flavour combined with the tangy fino, nutty amontillado or full-bodied oloroso make ideal partners.

PREPARATION AND COOKING TIME: **50 MINUTES**   SERVES **6**

250 g boiling potatoes, peeled and cut into even chunks | 2 tablespoons Spanish olive oil | 75 g chorizo *perilla*, skinned and finely diced | $^1/_2$ teaspoon cumin seeds | 50 g butter | 4 garlic cloves, peeled and sliced | 150 g drained weight of snails from a can (try to get them unpasteurised) | 1 tablespoon sherry vinegar | 1 tablespoon PX sherry | 5 tablespoons dark chicken jus | a handful of flat parsley leaves | salt and black pepper, to season

1 Put the potatoes into a pan of lightly salted water and bring to the boil. Simmer for 20 minutes until tender, drain and mash.

2 Meanwhile, heat the oil in a pan and cook the chorizo and cumin over a moderate heat for 5 minutes until the chorizo is cooked and beginning to stick to the pan.

3 Tip the chorizo and juices into the mash, mix well, season and keep warm.

4 In a frying pan melt the butter in a pan over a medium heat for a few minutes until it turns golden brown, then add the garlic and cook until it begins to caramelise. Add the snails and sauté for a minute, stirring often.

5 Add the sherry vinegar, sherry and chicken jus. Bring to the boil and simmer to reduce the liquid by half. Check seasoning and then stir in two thirds of the parsley.

6 To serve, divide the mash between 4 small bowl-plates, then top with the snails, drizzle over the cooking juices and scatter with the remaining parsley.

AMONTILLADO

TASTING NOTES Gentle and fresh with almonds on nosing, this pale straw coloured sherry is medium-bodied, with a hazelnutty palate. **SERVING TEMPERATURE** Best served slightly cooler than room temperature, so leave it in the fridge for roughly an hour before opening. **FOOD** Delicious with hot spicy foods and meats, including sticky BBQ ribs, chorizo sausage, Sunday roasts, Chinese chicken wings and dried ham. Amontillado is also said to go well with mature Cheddar, nuts, soups, olives, mushrooms, fried fish and desserts. **STORAGE** Although amontillado can be kept in an unopened bottle for up to three years, the flavour does eventually start to withdraw. It can be kept for up to a couple of weeks after opening, but it's best to finish the bottle relatively quickly.

DEEP-FRIED FROG'S LEGS & CHILLIES WITH BUTTERNUT COCONUT CURRY

Best paired with:
PALO CORTADO,
PALE CREAM,
CREAM

FROG'S LEGS INVARIABLY COME FROZEN FROM YOUR FISHMONGER. IF YOU CAN'T GET them use thick flakes of line-caught cod or some strips of sole. Guindilla chillies are pickled Spanish chillies – sweet and spicy. You could also use Turkish or any other good quality pickled chilli. The curry sauce is used much like a dipping sauce and you can make it as spicy or mild as you like – just add more or less chilli. Enjoy with a glass of cream or chilled sweet pale cream sherry.

PREPARATION AND COOKING TIME: **1 HOUR 30 MINUTES**   SERVES **8**

24 individual frog's legs (12 pairs) | 1 small red onion, thinly sliced | 500 ml peanut oil | 1 teaspoon Thai red curry paste (more or less to taste) | 1 teaspoon grated pale palm sugar or soft brown sugar | 1 teaspoon nam pla (fish sauce) | 200 g butternut squash, de-seeded, peeled and chopped | 2 tomatoes, skinned, de-seeded and chopped | 200 ml unsweetened coconut milk | 50 g roasted skinless peanuts | 8 guindilla chillies | 50 g plain flour | 50 g cornflour | 20 g baking powder | $^1/_4$ teaspoon salt | 1 quail's egg (or 1 egg white), beaten | 200 ml cold water | $^1/_2$ cucumber, peeled, de-seeded and diced | 3 spring onions, finely sliced | a handful of coriander leaves | salt, to season

1 To prepare the frogs legs you need to tunnel bone the thigh. The easiest way is to 'roll' the thigh meat back towards the knee joint, then cut the bone off just above the knee joint by firmly chopping it laid on a chopping board. Roll the meat back to its proper place then, using a small sharp knife, loosen the calf muscle meat and fold this back towards the thigh meat. At this point you will have a very slender calf bone and a gathering of meat hanging off the end of it. Set aside.

2 In a wide pan, fry the onion in 1 tablespoon of peanut oil for a few minutes. Add the curry paste and fry for 30 seconds, stirring constantly. Add the palm sugar and fish sauce and cook for 30 seconds, stirring constantly.

3 Add the butternut squash, tomatoes and coconut milk and bring to the boil. Cover and simmer for 15–20 minutes until the butternut is cooked, stirring occasionally. Stir in the peanuts, then whiz to a coarse purée in a food processor. Season to taste and keep warm.

4 Meanwhile, prick the chillies a few times with the point of a sharp knife and press between kitchen paper to absorb excess pickling liquid. Set aside.

5 To make the batter sift the flour, cornflour, baking powder and salt into a large bowl. Gradually whisk in the egg and water and leave to rest for 10 minutes. If it seems too thick, whisk it again and then add a little cold water.

6 Heat 4 cm of peanut oil in a wok to 180°C. Dip the frog's legs into the batter and deep-fry in batches of 6–8 at a time until golden and crisp – drain on kitchen paper and keep in a warm place while you cook the rest. Dip the chillies in the batter and deep-fry until golden.

7 To serve, divide the curry sauce amongst 8 bowls and then add the cucumber chunks. Scatter with the spring onions and half of the coriander, and then place 3 deep-fried legs and a deep-fried chilli on top. Garnish with the remaining coriander.

CHOCOLATE DELICE WITH
SHERRY PRUNES & VANILLA CREAM

THIS DELICE IS VERY RICH AND WILL KEEP IN THE FRIDGE FOR A WEEK AND TO BE HONEST it's hard to make in a small batch – this will make more than enough delice for 12–15 people but I've given quantities for 6 of everything else. It may seem odd to weigh the cream, milk and egg yolks, but it's more accurate in these smaller quantities. The creamy flavours marry perfectly with a glass of moscatel or Pedro Ximénez.

PREPARATION AND COOKING TIME: **30 MINUTES, PLUS 8 HOURS CHILLING**   SERVES **6**

12 prunes, stoned and halved | 150 ml cold water | 4 tablespoons PX sherry | 2 handfuls of raspberries | **FOR THE DELICE:** 75 g egg yolks | 100 g caster sugar | 300 g full fat milk | 250 g double cream | 200 g dark chocolate, chopped | 2 tablespoons PX sherry | **FOR THE VANILLA CREAM:** 200 ml double cream | 2 tablespoons vanilla sugar (or 2 tablespoons caster sugar and $1/4$ teaspoon pure vanilla extract)

1 Place the prunes in a small pan with the cold water. Bring to a simmer and cook for 5 minutes, gently stirring twice. Add the sherry and simmer for 2–3 minutes, until the cooking liquid thickens, then leave to cool. Chill, covered, in the fridge.

2 Meanwhile to make the delice, whisk the egg yolks with half the sugar until pale in colour. Place the remaining sugar in a pan with the milk and cream and bring to a simmer.

3 Pour the hot cream over the egg yolks, whisking continuously, then return to the pan and cook over a moderate heat, stirring constantly until the custard thickens and coats the back of the spoon.

4 Place the chocolate and sherry into a metal bowl, pour the hot custard mixture over and gently mix it together until the chocolate melts. Pour through a sieve into a clean bowl. Press some baking parchment on to the surface of the delice and leave to cool. Chill in the fridge for at least 8 hours to set.

5 To make the vanilla cream whisk the double cream and sugar until it forms soft peaks. Chill in the fridge.

6 To assemble, use 6 small glass bowls or martini glasses and place a raspberry or a few raspberries in the bottom of each. Divide the vanilla cream amongst them. Top each with a spoonful of cooked prunes and then a quenelle of the delice. Drizzle each dessert with a few teaspoons of the prune liquid.

TIP To quenelle the delice, half fill a heatproof jug with very hot water. Sit a dessertspoon in it to warm up – ideally a spoon with a half egg-shaped hollow. Run the hot and still slightly damp spoon across the top of the delice, slightly digging it in as you drag it along. The delice should roll up into the spoon and give you an egg-shaped quenelle.

MICHAEL CAINES WORKED UNDER INFLUENTIAL CHEFS Raymond Blanc, Bernard Loiseau and Joël Robuchon before taking up the position of head chef at *Gidleigh Park* in Devon in 1994. Only two months into the job, Michael suffered a terrible car accident in which he lost his right arm. Remarkably, he was back in the kitchen within two weeks more focused and determined than ever to pursue his dream of reaching the top of his profession. Michael has created a style that is uniquely his own, at once classic yet also highly innovative, a fact recognised with the award of a second Michelin star in 1999. He has opened restaurants at the Royal Clarence Hotel in Exeter and the Bristol Marriott Royal, and is operating partner for Abode Hotels.

"There is a new vogue for sherry, both dry and cream. It deserves recognition."

Michael is a fan of the Spanish-style of eating and believes that putting food in the middle of the table for everyone to share is a great way to eat. Like many of us, his first taste of cream sherry was eating trifle as a boy but nowadays he is much more likely to enjoy it in many other ways, from drinking it alongside the start of his meal right through to serving it with blue cheese as a dessert wine.

EXOTIC FRUIT BROCHETTE
WITH COCONUT RICE
PUDDING & SHERRY SABAYON

Best paired with:
CREAM,
PEDRO XIMÉNEZ

CREAMY RICE PUDDING TOPPED WITH FRESH FRUITS – SIMPLY DIVINE, ESPECIALLY WHEN served with a cream sherry. Soak the wooden skewers in cold water for at least 30 minutes before cooking. To make stock syrup put 50 g granulated sugar in a pan and pour over 100 ml warm water. Brush the sides of the pan with water to rinse away any sugar. Gently heat until the sugar has dissolved and then boil for 2 minutes. Allow to cool and then use.

PREPARATION TIME: **20 MINUTES** COOKING TIME: **40 MINUTES** SERVES **4**

$1/2$ mango, peeled and stoned | $1/2$ pineapple, peeled and cored | $1/2$ paw paw, peeled and de-seeded | 1 kiwi fruit, peeled | 4 lychees, peeled | 100 g pudding rice | 600 ml full fat milk | 1 vanilla pod, split in half | 25 g desiccated coconut | 100 g caster sugar | 4 egg yolks | 100 ml stock syrup | 125 ml double cream, whipped | 2 tablespoons cream sherry

1 Cut the mango, pineapple, paw paw and kiwi into 2 cm cubes. Thread the fruit, including the lychees, on to 4 soaked wooden skewers, alternating different types. Place on a grill tray and set aside.

2 Blanch the rice in boiling water for 2–3 minutes, then drain. Heat the milk, vanilla, coconut and sugar in a pan just to the boil. Add the blanched rice and simmer for 30 minutes, stirring occasionally until thick and the liquid has been absorbed. Divide amongst four 7 x 4 cm mini loaf tins.

3 Meanwhile, whisk together the egg yolks and the stock syrup in a bowl over a pan of barely simmering water until thick. Allow to cool and then fold in the whipped cream and sherry.

4 Preheat the grill to hot and grill the fruit skewers lightly to warm through, turning.

5 To serve, unmould the rice puddings on to four plates and top each with a fruit brochette. Add the sabayon and serve.

MARK JANKEL

AFTER ONLY EIGHT MONTHS AT CHEF SCHOOL MARK JANKEL talked his way into a job at Phillip Howard's two Michelin-starred restaurant, *The Square*. After two years he moved to work as sous chef under Jun Tanaka, first at *QC*, then at *Pearl,* all in London. Mark has been head chef of *Notting Hill Brasserie* for three years.

"Having thought of a dish, it is pretty straightforward to choose a sherry style that will work well with it. You should be able to taste the sherry and dish at the same time, neither one being dominant. There will be plenty of variance within each style, every sherry has its own personality and charm."

Mark has some pretty specific ideas on matching sherry with food — not surprising considering he and his sommelier Patrice Guillon won the esteemed gastronomic challenge Copa Jerez in 2005 for their menu and sherry pairings. He considers sherry more stable and consistent than other wines and therefore more trustworthy in terms of food and wine matching. He really enjoys seeing his friends tasting the connection between food and wine.

ROAST SQUAB & LOBSTER OPEN PASTA PARCELS

Best paired with:
AMONTILLADO,
OLOROSO,
PALO CORTADO

HOME-MADE PASTA IS SIMPLY DIVINE. YOU MUST USE PASTA FLOUR CALLED '00'. IT IS A strong, very finely milled flour that produces smooth and silky pasta and is available from most good supermarkets. To help subdue the lobster, try chilling it in the freezer for a few hours. A squab is a fledgling pigeon and is very tender and succulent and is in season all year round. Enjoy with dry oloroso.

PREPARATION TIME: **45 MINUTES** COOKING TIME: **2 HOURS 20 MINUTES** SERVES **8**

4 small native lobsters | 2 carrots, roughly chopped | 1 onion, roughly chopped | 4 squab pigeons | 2 eggs | 200 g pasta flour | 2 tablespoons olive oil

1 Bring a pan of water just to the boil. Plunge in the lobster and cook for 3 minutes. Then refresh in ice water.

2 Remove the lobster tails and claws and reserve. Keep the remaining shells but discard the guts. Allow the meat in the tails and claws to cool, and then chill.

3 To make a lobster stock put the lobster shells, carrot and onion in a large pan and cover with water. Bring to the boil and simmer for 2 hours.

4 Preheat the oven to Gas Mark 6/200°C/400°F. Pass the stock through a fine sieve and then rapidly boil until reduced by two thirds, skimming the surface often. Pass through a fine sieve and keep on a simmer.

5 Roast the pigeons in the oven for 20 minutes. Allow to rest for about 10 minutes.

6 Meanwhile, put the eggs, flour and 2 teaspoons olive oil in a food mixer with a dough hook and mix until a smooth dough. Roll the pasta into thin sheets using a pasta machine and cut into 8 rectangles.

7 Remove the pigeon breast meat from the bone and keep warm. Sauté the lobster tail and claws in the remaining olive oil for a few minutes. Cut in half and keep warm. Increase the lobster stock to the boil, add the pasta rectangles and cook for 3 minutes.

8 Wrap a length of pasta around a pigeon breast, half a lobster tail and a claw and put on a plate. Repeat this with the other breasts, tails and claws. Whiz the remaining lobster stock with a hand blender, then spoon over the pasta parcels and serve.

SAUTÉ OF SCALLOP, PORK BELLY, BLACK PUDDING & WILD MUSHROOMS

Best paired with:
AMONTILLADO,
PALO CORTADO

FOUR LITTLE MOUTHFULS OF HEAVEN, THESE ARE EVEN BETTER WHEN SERVED WITH A glass of amontillado.

PREPARATION TIME: **15 MINUTES** COOKING TIME: **3 HOURS** SERVES **8**

400 g organic pork belly | 100 g butter | 300 g celeriac, peeled and chopped into small cubes | 100 ml double cream | 300 g mixed wild mushrooms | 2 shallots, diced | 1 tomato, de-seeded and diced | $^1/_2$ bunch of chives, snipped | 300 g black pudding, cut into eight 4 cm slices | 8 large scallops

1 Preheat the oven to Gas Mark $^1/_2$/130°C/ 250°F. Slow roast the pork belly for about 3 hours until the meat is very tender.

2 After 2 hours 15 minutes melt 50 g butter in a pan and add the celeriac. Cover with a piece of baking parchment and cook gently for 20 minutes until tender.

3 Add the cream and cook until the cream starts to thicken. Whiz in a blender and then push through a fine sieve. Return to a clean pan and keep warm.

4 Gently fry the wild mushrooms in the remaining butter for a few minutes. Add the shallots and cook for a further 3–4 minutes. Stir in the tomato and cook for a further few minutes. Stir in the chives and keep warm.

5 Preheat the grill to hot. Cut the pork belly into eight 4 cm cubes and keep warm. Grill the black pudding for a few minutes, turning, then keep warm.

6 Sauté the scallops in a hot pan for 60 seconds on each side. To serve, divide the scallops, pork belly, black pudding and wild mushrooms, (shaped in a small ring mould) in a row on the plates. Drizzle each black pudding with a little celeriac purée and serve.

"This dish is a bit challenging in terms of wine matching as it has substantial variance in flavours. However, all the flavours are quite earthy, rich and creamy. This dish needs a more mature, deeper and grown up amontillado. A 30-year-old amontillado with an aged confident intensity and warm roasted character would support the flavours of the dish rather than balance them."

CRISPY LAMB ROLLS WITH CARAMELISED SWEETBREADS

Best paired with:
AMONTILLADO,
MEDIUM

THINLY SLICED LAMB RUMP WITH BRAISED SHOULDER, CARAMELISED SWEETBREADS AND mint dressing. The long cooking time of the lamb allows the meat to be really tender and melt-in-the mouth. Serve with a nutty amontillado.

PREPARATION TIME: **40 MINUTES** COOKING TIME: 3½ **HOURS** SERVES **4–6**

30 g butter | 6 tablespoons olive oil | 500 g lamb shoulder | 2 carrots, chopped | 1 onion, chopped | 3 litres chicken stock | 2 organic lamb rumps (or a piece of lamb chump) | 1 bunch of mint | 50 ml sweet white vinegar | 1 packet spring roll pastry | 1 egg white, lightly whisked | 200 g lamb sweetbreads, membrane removed | salt and black pepper, to season

1 Heat 25 g butter and 2 tablespoons oil in a pan and brown the lamb shoulder on all sides. Remove and set aside. Add the carrot and onion and cook for 3–4 minutes until softened.

2 Return the lamb shoulder to the pan, cover with chicken stock and cook on a very low heat for about 3 hours. Allow to cool and then remove the lamb shoulder from the stock and set aside. Bring the stock to the boil and reduce until it becomes sticky, then remove from the heat. Meanwhile, shred the meat from the lamb shoulder. Mix the shredded meat into the sticky stock reduction.

3 Preheat the oven to Gas Mark 2/150°C/300°F. Roast the lamb rumps in the oven until medium rare. The best way to check is to use a thin skewer. Insert it into the centre of the meat at intervals as the meat cooks. Remove the skewer and carefully press it against your lip. As the meat starts to cook the internal temperature will rise and it will feel warmer against your lip. When it just starts to get hot, take the meat out and let it rest, it should be medium rare. Once cool, chill in the fridge.

4 Meanwhile, whiz the mint leaves with the vinegar in a blender until smooth. Season to taste and chill. Lay the pastry on a work surface, brush with a little egg white, and spoon the shredded lamb shoulder in a line across the sheet of pastry. Roll up the pastry to make a cylinder with the braised lamb in the middle. Seal at both ends with egg white.

5 Heat 2 tablespoons olive oil in a pan and fry the lamb roll for 5 minutes until crispy and golden. Remove and cut into 6 slices. Keep warm.

6 Heat the remaining olive oil in another pan and fry the sweetbreads until golden and crispy on one side, add the remaining butter, turn over the sweetbreads and cook for another few minutes.

7 To serve, slice the lamb as thinly as possible (for a special occasion trim into a rectangle) and arrange on a plate. Spoon the mint dressing on top and then arrange the sweetbreads and crispy lamb rolls.

DEEP FRIED LANGOUSTINE WITH ROASTED PROVENÇAL VEGETABLES & VIOLET ARTICHOKES

Best paired with:
FINO

MAKE SURE YOU GET REALLY FRESH LANGOUSTINES FROM A GOOD FISHMONGER. THEY ARE also known as Dublin bay prawns, scampi or Norway lobsters. The delicious rich lobster bisque should be served on the side with a chilled glass of crisp, dry fino.

PREPARATION TIME: **45 MINUTES** COOKING TIME: **2¹/₂ HOURS** SERVES **4**

12 live langoustines | 50 g plain flour | 1 egg, beaten | 250 g fresh breadcrumbs | 2 carrots, diced | 1 onion, diced | 1 tomato | 2 sprigs of basil | juice of 2 lemons | 4 violet or baby artichoke hearts | 75 ml olive oil | 1 aubergine, thinly sliced | 2 courgettes, thinly sliced | 2 red peppers, de-seeded and thinly sliced | 1 fennel, outer leaves removed and thinly sliced | ¹/₂ bunch chives, snipped | 1 shallot, finely diced | vegetable oil, for deep-frying | salt, to season

1 Blanch the langoustines in boiling water for 60 seconds. Remove the tail and the tail meat from the shell and keep along with the rest of the shells. Roll the langoustine tail meat in the flour, then the egg and then the breadcrumbs. Chill surrounded by extra breadcrumbs.

2 Make a soup by placing the shells, carrots, onion, tomato and basil in a pan and just covering with water. Simmer for about 2 hours and then pass through a sieve. Return to the pan and boil rapidly until reduced slightly. Season with salt and a squeeze of lemon juice and keep warm.

3 Bring a pan of water to the boil and season with salt and juice of one lemon. Plunge in the artichokes and simmer for 10 minutes or until tender. Allow to cool in the cooking liquid, then drain and cut the artichokes in quarters lengthways.

4 Meanwhile, brush the aubergines, courgettes, pepper and fennel with a little of the olive oil and griddle for 5–10 minutes in batches until cooked. Season with salt and keep warm.

5 Dress the artichokes with the remaining olive oil, chives, shallot and lemon juice. Set aside.

6 Heat the vegetable oil in a pan until a cube of bread browns in 60 seconds. Deep-fry the langoustines, in batches, until golden. Drain on kitchen paper and season.

7 Arrange the grilled vegetables on a plate. Lay the artichokes and langoustines on top and serve the soup on the side.

TIP For a really professional finish, layer the griddled vegetables in a loaf tin lined with cling film, then place in the freezer for a few hours until semi-frozen. Unwrap and, working very carefully, slice the terrine using a serrated knife. Arrange on the serving plates.

"The sweet luxurious flesh of the langoustine together with the slightly acidic artichokes and lightly caramelised vegetables balance perfectly with an ice-cold, crisp dry fino. A fino works really well as it stands up to the richness of the langoustine and the acidity of the artichokes."

POACHED PEAR MILLEFEUILLE WITH PEAR SORBET

Best paired with:
SWEET OLOROSO,
CREAM

FOR A CHEAT'S VERSION USE READY-MADE, GOOD QUALITY SORBET. MILLEFEUILLE MEANS a thousand layers, which is what puff pastry is made of — lots of layers. Delicious with a glass of cream sherry.

PREPARATION AND COOKING TIME: **50 MINUTES, PLUS FREEZING**   SERVES **4**

150 g icing sugar | 300 g puff pastry | 600 g good quality pear sorbet | **FOR THE POACHED PEARS:** 500 g sugar | I litre cold water | 4 star anise | 2 cinnamon sticks | 1 orange, quartered | 4 ripe pears, peeled and cored | **FOR THE CUSTARD:** 125 g caster sugar | 250 ml milk | 250 ml double cream | 6 star anise | 6 egg yolks

1 To poach the pears, put the sugar, water, star anises, cinnamon sticks and orange pieces in a pan and gently heat until the sugar dissolves. Bring to a simmer and add the pears. Cook for 5–10 minutes until the pears are tender. Remove and allow to cool.

2 To make the custard put 50 g sugar, the milk, cream and star anise in a pan and bring to the boil. Meanwhile, whisk the yolks with the remaining sugar until pale.

3 Gradually stir the hot milk liquid into the egg yolks until smooth. Return to a clean pan and gently heat on a very low heat, stirring constantly until it thickens. Remove from the heat, strain through a fine sieve and chill.

4 Preheat the oven to Gas Mark 4/180°C/350°F. Dust some icing sugar on to a clean surface and roll the puff pastry until it is extremely thin. You have to be very patient, as the pastry becomes moist, so repeatedly dust with icing sugar and turn over.

5 Cook the pastry between two baking trays in the oven for about 5 minutes or until golden. While the pastry is still hot, cut out 8 discs that are the same diameter as the base of the pear. Then cut another 4 a bit smaller and repeat until you have 20 discs decreasing in size.

6 Slice the pears horizontally into six pieces and insert a puff pastry disc in between each slice of pear. Place a pear at the end of a plate, a spoonful of the pear sorbet on a pastry disc in the middle and the custard at the other end.

OLOROSO

TASTING NOTES A dark amber or mahogany colour and medium- to full-bodied, there's plenty of walnut to both the nose and on the palate. Naturally dry, sweeter versions are also available. **SERVING TEMPERATURE** Room temperature, slightly chilled or on the rocks with a slice of lime or orange...experiment until you find a combination that works for you. **FOOD** The drier varieties of oloroso with nuts, fresh fruit, black pudding, smoked sausages, offal, red meat and game. Sweeter versions try with fruit, dried fruit and desserts such as bread and butter pudding, gingerbread, crème brûlée and treacle tart.

VICKY BHOGAL

VICKY BHOGAL'S FIRST BOOK *COOKING LIKE MUMMYJI* received rave reviews. It takes a fresh look at real British Asian home cooking and culture, exploding a few myths and stereotypes along the way! *A Year Of Cooking Like Mummyji*, published three years later, covers seasonal Indian cooking and features a number of Fairtrade recipes, a foundation for which she is a spokesperson.

Robust and strongly flavoured sherries are an interesting accompaniment for traditional Asian food as both sherry and food can hold their own, creating a memorable eating experience.

CORIANDER CHICKEN TIKKA

THESE LITTLE GOUJONS OF CHICKEN ARE A MATCH MADE IN HEAVEN WITH OLOROSO. THE WARM, medium to full-bodied sherry complements the spiciness of these tasty, tender chicken mouthfuls which are simplicity itself to prepare.

PREPARATION TIME: **15 MINUTES, PLUS 4 HOURS MARINATING**
COOKING TIME: **30 MINUTES**   SERVES **4**

4 green chillies | 1 teaspoon ground turmeric | 2 tablespoons whole coriander seeds
| 2 teaspoons ground coriander | 2 large handfuls of chopped coriander | 2 teaspoons garam masala | 6 garlic cloves | 1 small onion, roughly chopped | 1 tablespoon grated ginger
| 1 tablespoon natural yoghurt | 2 tablespoons lemon juice | 4 tablespoons mild olive oil
| 1 teaspoon salt | 450 g boneless chicken breast goujons or mini fillets

1 Place all the ingredients, except the chicken, in a blender or grinder and whiz to a thick paste. Massage the chicken with the paste, cover and marinate in the fridge for at least 4 hours.

2 Preheat the oven to Gas Mark 4/180ºC/ 375ºF. Shake off any excess marinade and place the chicken on a baking tray. Roast for 30 minutes, turning over halfway through. Serve immediately or eat cold.

GINGER LAMB CHOPS

Best paired with:
OLOROSO,
CREAM

THE SUCCULENT LAMB COATED IN FRAGRANT SPICES WORKS REALLY WELL WITH A CREAM sherry and is perfect eaten as a small snack on its own or make a meal of it and serve with some warm bread. You can use French trimmed lamb chops instead of the cutlets if you prefer.

PREPARATION TIME: **15 MINUTES** COOKING TIME: **1 HOUR 15 MINUTES**   SERVES **4**

2 teaspoons finely chopped garlic | 3 tablespoons grated ginger| 4 tablespoons vegetable oil | 450 g tomatoes, de-seeded and finely chopped| 4 lamb cutlets | 1 teaspoon salt | $^1/_2$ teaspoon red chilli powder | $^1/_2$ teaspoon ground turmeric | 600 ml boiling water| 25 g butter | $^1/_4$ red onion, very thinly sliced, 1 spring onion, very finely chopped and a handful of chopped fresh

1 Purée the garlic and 1 tablespoon of the ginger in a mini blender or by pounding in a pestle and mortar until finely crushed. Heat the oil in a saucepan and add the ginger and garlic. Fry until a deep golden brown.

2 Reduce the heat and add the tomatoes. Fry for about a minute.

3 Add the chops, salt, red chilli powder, turmeric and boiling water. Stir well and cook on a low heat, covered, for 50 minutes. Remove the lid and increase the heat to evaporate any excess water, stirring frequently.

4 Turn the heat down low and keep stirring until the oil separates from the sauce. The sauce should be really quite thick.

5 Add the remaining ginger and butter. Stir and cook uncovered for about 4 minutes. Garnish with the red onion, spring onion and coriander.

WATERMELON, FETA & GARAM MASALA SKEWERS

Best paired with:
MANZANILLA,
FINO,
PALE CREAM

FRESH AND LIGHT, THESE SPICY SKEWERS ARE DELICIOUS WITH MANZANILLA AND HAVE a real kick to them. Make them up to a few hours in advance.

PREPARATION TIME: **20 MINUTES**   SERVES 8–10

$^1/_2$ small watermelon | 200 g feta cheese | $^1/_2$ teaspoon garam masala | $^1/_2$ teaspoon ground cumin | 1 tablespoon extra virgin olive oil | $^1/_4$ teaspoon red chilli powder | dash of lime juice | 1 teaspoon freeze dried chopped coriander leaf | salt and black pepper, to season

1 Cut the watermelon into bite size chunks, discarding the peel and any obvious seeds.

2 Cut the feta into chunks of a similar size to the watermelon and place in a bowl. Add the remaining ingredients and stir well to coat.

3 Thread the watermelon and feta chunks on to medium size skewers and serve.

MANZANILLA

TASTING NOTES Pale in colour, manzanilla is a dry and very light wine with salt, apple and yeast on the nose. **SERVING TEMPERATURE** Well chilled. **FOOD** Not a million miles away from fino, manzanilla is particularly well coupled with fish and chips and other main fish courses. It's also great with salted almonds, green olives, soups, cheeses and spicy snacks. Try using a nice dry manzanilla in sauces as an alternative to sake or white wine. The flavour is light but aromatic. **STORAGE** Thanks to modern bottling techniques a good sherry can now be stored for at least 18 months. However, it is advisable to drink the lighter fino and manzanilla sherries within a couple of months of purchase to get the most from their delicate flavours. Once open keep them refrigerated and consume within a week.

ALOO TIKKI BITES

Best paired with:
FINO,
AMONTILLADO,
DRY OLOROSO

THESE ARE LITTLE MOUTHFULS OF ABSOLUTE PLEASURE. ALOO MEANS POTATO, WHICH is what binds all the spices together – they go sensationally well with a glass of fino. You should be able to find gram flour in good Indian supermarkets.

PREPARATION TIME: **20 MINUTES, PLUS 30 MINUTES CHILLING**
COOKING TIME: **30 MINUTES**   MAKES **26**

1 tablespoon oil | 2 teaspoons cumin seeds | $^1/_2$ onion, thinly sliced | 2 teaspoons lemon juice | 1 teaspoon garam masala | $1^1/_2$ teaspoons salt | 1 teaspoon dried red chilli flakes | a handful of finely chopped coriander | 4 potatoes, peeled, boiled and mashed | 150 g gram flour | vegetable oil for frying

1 Heat the oil in a frying pan and add the cumin seeds. When sizzling, add the onion and fry until translucent.

2 Add the lemon juice, garam masala, salt, chilli and coriander and stir well for about a minute

3 Switch off the heat and add the mashed potato to the pan. Mash well with the spices. Place in a bowl and chill for 30 minutes.

4 Meanwhile, place the gram flour in a bowl and add enough water, by adding slowly and stirring continuously, to make a thick smooth batter.

5 Roll the potato mixture into 26 little balls. In a large pan, heat vegetable oil until a cube of bread browns in 30 seconds. Coat each little ball generously with the batter and deep-fry in batches for about 4 minutes until golden all over. Drain on kitchen paper and serve.

CARROT & MAPLE SYRUP HALWA

Best paired with:
CREAM,
PEDRO XIMÉNEZ

HALWA IS INTENSELY SWEET AND GOES REALLY WELL WITH A GLASS OF PEDRO XIMENÉZ. HALWA IS traditionally a dessert or sweet, which you may find surprising as it uses carrots as the main base — but once you've tried it you won't look back.

PREPARATION AND COOKING TIME: **50 MINUTES**   SERVES 4–6

10 large carrots, peeled and grated | 7 tablespoons butter | 5 cloves | 6 green cardamoms, crushed | 1 cinnamon stick | 250 ml milk | 250 g granulated sugar | 2 tablespoons maple syrup | desiccated coconut, to serve

1 Bring a pan of water to the boil. Add the carrots and simmer for 10 minutes. Drain into a colander.

2 Melt the butter in a pan with the cloves, cardamom and cinnamon on a very low heat. Add the milk and stir well.

3 When the cardamom begins to release its fragrant scent, add the sugar.

4 Stir until the sugar has dissolved and then add the carrots. Cover and gently cook through on a very low heat for 15 minutes until the liquid has dried.

5 Add the maple syrup and stir through before serving. Sprinkle with desiccated coconut to serve.

AT 37, ANGELA HARTNETT HAS BECOME ONE OF THE MOST high profile women in the restaurant world. After launching *Amaryllis* in Scotland 2001, Angela turned her attention to the launch of Gordon Ramsay's *Verre* in Dubai. She returned to England to open *Menu* and *The Grill Room* at The Connaught where she combines great British cuisine with a modern European influence. Since taking up the position at The Connaught, Angela has gone from strength to strength and in January 2004 won her first Michelin star.

"I really love sherry when I am eating tapas..."

Angela relishes tapas because they are a great way of making food a shared experience – and she loves to drink sherry when she is eating them. She enjoys the experience so much she has introduced a tapas menu to the Terrace at The Connaught.

GRILLED SALT COD ON CROSTINI WITH PICKLED VEGETABLES

Best paired with:
FINO,
PALE CREAM

THE SWEET BUT LIGHT TASTE OF A PALE CREAM SHERRY PERFECTLY COMPLEMENTS THE salt cod. You can also serve this dish with crushed new potatoes for a more substantial meal.

PREPARATION TIME: **10 MINUTES, PLUS 24 HOURS SOAKING** COOKING TIME: **45 MINUTES**
SERVES **4**

400 g salt cod | 150 ml cold water | 4 tablespoons white wine vinegar | 3 wild garlic cloves, crushed | juice of 1 lemon | 1 teaspoon coriander seeds, crushed | 1 tablespoon fresh thyme leaves | 125 ml olive oil | 1 courgette, diced | 1 aubergine, diced | 1 pepper, de-seeded and diced | 4 slices baguette | 100 ml dry white wine | 50 g capers, finely chopped, plus 4 whole caper berries to garnish | 50 g gherkins, finely chopped, plus 4 whole gherkins to garnish | 75 g black olives, roughly chopped | 1 tablespoons chopped flat leaf parsley | 4 chives, to garnish

1 Put the salt cod in a large container and cover with cold water. Chill for 24 hours, changing the water 4 or 5 times.

2 Put the water, vinegar, garlic, lemon juice, coriander seeds and thyme in a pan. Bring to the boil and simmer for 15 minutes.

3 Stir in half the oil, the courgette, aubergine and pepper. Cook for 15 minutes or until just tender. Drain in a sieve.

4 Preheat the grill to hot. Toast the baguette slices on both sides until golden. Set aside. Drain the cod and pat dry, then place under the grill for 8–10 minutes until cooked. Meanwhile, heat a pan with the remaining olive oil, when hot add the white wine, capers and gherkins. Bubble for a few minutes to warm through then stir in the cooked vegetables, olives and parsley.

5 Divide the vegetables between 4 plates (using a ring mould if you wish), top with the toasted baguette and salt cod. Garnish each plate with a whole caper berry and gherkin and drizzle dressing around. Garnish with chives.

JEREZ: THE SHERRY TRIANGLE

Three towns in the rolling white hills of southwest Spain encapsulate a sherry kingdom. Jerez de la Frontera, Puerto de Santa María and Sanlúcar de Barrameda mark out the 'sherry triangle', home to festivals, flamenco and, of course, sherry.

It's all about climate and soil. Jerez may be one of the hottest winemaking regions in the world, just a hop, skip and a jump from the coast of North Africa, but it enjoys cooling, Atlantic sea breezes. The combination of searing heat and tempering, briny wind helps the flor to grow – the layer of yeast that grows on the wine in the cask, which gives the wine its individual character.

The soil is another major factor. The best has the ability to hang on to what little rain the region gets: drying without cracking, sealing in and slowly releasing moisture to the deep-rooted vines during the long cloudless summer days. Called albariza, its dazzling whiteness in the sun is due to the large proportion of chalk, with the best plots nearest the sea.

Sherry from the Sherry Triangle

The unique flavour of individual sherries depends on the microclimates found in the three major sherry-producing towns of the sherry triangle – and sometimes even within a single bodega. It is only after the grapes are harvested, pressed and fermented that the real work of the bodegas begins, choosing which wines will become finos (or manzanillas from Sanlúcar), which olorosos – or amontillados if the flor dies naturally. Then ageing follows and blending with the naturally sweet grapes of PX or moscatel to produce cream, pale cream, medium and palo cortado.

Jerez is the centre of sherry production, and positioned the furthest inland of the three key towns – temperatures here reach

30–40˚C in summer. The bodegas are positioned to benefit from any cooling maritime breezes that reach the town, nevertheless the wines produced in this heat are full-bodied and bold.

Sanlúcar de Barrameda is the only place that makes manzanilla. The town is cooler than Jerez. The iodine-laden wind whips off the sea, and humidity is generated from the vast pine-clad nature reserve, the Coto Doñana, just across the water – all of which the flor thrives on. Many claim that manzanilla has a saltier tang than fino.

"We have to thank the Moors for the name 'sherry' as they named the town Seris and this was later adapted to Jerez."

El Puerto de Santa María is positioned midway between Cádiz and Jerez. Only about five per cent of sherry is made here – but the style is different again. Wines from El Puerto are a tad lighter and more delicate than the others. This is because, except for a large promontory, the town takes the brunt of Atlantic gusts, making it a few degrees cooler than Jerez and less humid than Sanlúcar.

A History of Jerez

The Jerez region has had a turbulent history. First the Phoenicians moved in, founding the port of Cádiz, then the Carthaginians, who were succeeded by the Romans, Vandals and Visigoths.

The Moors who followed had the longest run as rulers, remaining for seven centuries. Their influence can be seen and felt in many aspects of Andalucían life, not least in the architecture, and we have to thank them for the name 'sherry' as they named the town Seris and this was later adapted to Jerez. Then after the Moors came the Christians. Amazingly, wine continued to be made here pretty much throughout.

Export to England began sometime during the first half of the fourteenth century and increased during the latter part of the fifteenth, when Spain and England were allied by the marriage of Henry VIII to Catherine of Aragon.

Later, Sir Francis Drake, who was initially a merchant in Jerez, attacked Cádiz and made off with supplies intended for the Spanish Armada, including nearly 3,000 casks of sherry. These ended up on the English market just as the popularity of the drink was growing, and by the middle of the seventeenth century, sherry was *de rigueur* right across Europe.

When Spain's Catholic monarchs chucked out the Jews, they were succeeded by English, Breton and Genoese merchants in Jerez. By the late eighteenth century, English, Scottish and Irish merchants had arrived in force, some of their names living on today: Osborne, Sandeman and Williams & Humbert, to name a few.

Today, the industry is dominated by three major players: Beam Global which includes the category leader Harveys; González-Byass, which includes Tio Pepe; and the ever-expanding Medina Group, with Williams & Humbert. Other big names include Osborne, Caballero (owner of Lustau), Barbadillo and José Estévez (owner of Valdespino).

ICHIRO KUBOTA

ORIGINALLY FROM KYOTO, ICHIRO KUBOTA MOVED TO London in January 2004 to set up *Umu*, the UK's first Kyoto-style restaurant. Kubota spent seven years perfecting his skills in Japanese cuisine before moving to France to the Michelin-starred *Hotel La Villa* in Corsica. He spent a year working his way around the kitchen, studying techniques before short spells at *Duverger* in Lyons and the three-starred *Georges Blanc*. His next stop was London where his focus at *Umu* is on introducing classic and re-invented true Kyoto cuisine to London, drawing on the best of ingredients and techniques.

> **"Amontillado has similar aromas to Japanese red rice sake and a profound taste, it pairs perfectly with grilled meat."**

Kubota is fascinated by matching the sharp, dry flavours of Jerez finos and manzanillas with the pure flavours of the freshest ingredients. Here, he has experimented with the full range of sherries to match a traditional Kyoto grazing menu.

POPPY SEED TUNA WITH JAPANESE PLUM SAUCE

Best paired with:
PALE CREAM

SUCCULENT CHUNKS OF FRESH TUNA COATED IN CRUNCHY SEEDS, TOPPED WITH TART pink grapefruit and drizzled with sour and salty pickled plum sauce. The sauce is available in good Asian supermarkets. Combine with the medium sweetness of a pale cream sherry.

PREPARATION AND COOKING TIME: **15 MINUTES**   SERVES **6**

250 g fresh tuna steak | 1 egg white, lightly beaten | 40 g poppy seeds | $^1/_2$ tablespoon olive oil | 12 shiso or coriander leaves | $^1/_4$ pink grapefruit, segmented | cashew nut slivers | Japanese pickled plum sauce to serve

1 Brush the tuna with egg white and sprinkle all over with the poppy seeds.

2 Heat the oil in a non-stick frying pan until hot and sear the tuna for 3 minutes on each side. Allow to cool slightly.

3 Cut the tuna into 5 cm pieces. Fill six martini glasses with crushed ice and add a shiso or coriander leaf, top with the tuna and add another leaf. Place a pink grapefruit segment on top and two cashew nut slivers and serve with the Japanese plum sauce.

"For its similar taste and aroma to German whites, pale cream goes with this tuna dish which is clear in acidity and fresh in aroma."

AJI SUSHI

AJI IS A SMALL FISH CALLED HORSE MACKEREL. IF YOU CAN'T FIND AJI, SALMON OR TUNA work just as well. Kombu is kelp seaweed and is used to add flavour to the sushi rice. It is available from good Japanese supermarkets or health food shops. Manzanilla makes a refreshing accompaniment.

PREPARATION TIME: **45 MINUTES**   COOKING TIME: **15 MINUTES**
MAKES ABOUT **15 SUSHI ROLLS**

200 g sushi rice | 220 ml cold water | 5 g kombu | 100 ml rice vinegar | 55 g caster sugar | pinch of salt | 200 g aji horse mackerel fish, filleted and cut into 5 cm slices | seaweed, for wrapping | rice vinegar, for brushing | light soy sauce, for dipping

1 Put the rice, water and kombu in a heavy-based pan. Bring to the boil, cover and simmer for 15 minutes. Turn off the heat, keep the lid on and leave for a further 15 minutes.

2 Meanwhile, to make the sushi vinegar mix together in a jug the rice vinegar and the caster sugar. Season with a pinch of salt. Set aside.

3 Place the cooked rice in a large, shallow dish. Sprinkle with half the sushi vinegar and fold into the rice. Continue to add the sushi vinegar, using a piece of card to fan the rice to cool it down. When the rice reaches room temperature, cover with a damp cloth.

4 Press the rice into small rectangles and top each with a slice of mackerel. Brush the seaweed with rice vinegar then cut into strips and wrap a strip around each sushi. Serve with a dipping sauce of light soy sauce.

"Manzanilla's character and origin is close to the sea, it goes with seafood with saltiness and acidity. This is the perfect pairing to Kyoto-style stick sushi with horse mackerel in white seaweed and pickled ginger."

EEL YAKITORI

Best paired with:
FINO

YAKITORI MEANS 'JAPANESE GRILLED KEBABS', WHICH IN A WAY THESE ARE – SKEWERED pieces of eel glazed in sake and soy sauce. Bonito is basically a type of fish stock that you can find from good Japanese supermarkets, but if you can't buy it then use normal fish stock. Wasabi is a hot paste, something like horseradish, which is available from good supermarkets. Ask your fishmonger to clean and fillet the eel. Serve with a chilled, dry fino.

PREPARATION AND COOKING TIME: **15 MINUTES** SERVES **4–6**

100 ml dark soy sauce | 40 ml bonito or fish stock | 20 ml light soy sauce | 20 ml sake | 500 g eel fillets, cut into 2.5 cm pieces | wasabi and pickled ginger, to serve

1 For the dipping sauce mix together the dark soy sauce and 1 tablespoon fish stock in a bowl. Set aside.

2 In another bowl mix together the remaining fish stock, light soy sauce and sake. Skewer the eel pieces to keep it flat and brush with the marinade.Grill for 5-8 minutes under a medium-hot grill, turning and basting with the marinade until the skin becomes crispy and the eel is cooked.

3 Remove from the skewers and arrange on a plate. Serve with ginger and wasabi.

"Fino's sharpness in acidity and dryness goes with salted or simply grilled fish, sake flavoured grilled wild eel from Ireland with rock salt served with grated fresh wasabi."

GRILLED AUBERGINE WITH RED MISO

Best paired with:
AMONTILLADO,
OLOROSO,
PALO CORTADO

RED MISO IS MADE FROM WHITE RICE, BARLEY OR SOYA BEANS BY A NATURAL fermentation, which takes about one to three years. Mirin is a rice wine often used in Japanese cooking. You can find both in Japanese supermarkets, online or in good supermarkets. Baby aubergines could also work well for this dish. Try a spicy oloroso with this dish.

PREPARATION AND COOKING TIME: **25 MINUTES**   SERVES **4**

1 small aubergine | 2 tablespoons mild olive oil | 150 g red miso | 1 tablespoon mirin | 1 tablespoon sake | 2 tablespoons sesame paste (tahini) | 1 tablespoon caster sugar | 1 tablespoon white poppy seeds | fresh young ginger, to garnish | pickled Japanese sweet radishes, to serve

1 Cut the aubergine in 4 thick rounds and leave to soak in salted water for 5 minutes. Dry with kitchen paper.

2 Preheat the grill to medium. Prick a few holes in the skin around each slice and brush all over with olive oil. Grill for 10 minutes, turning.

3 Meanwhile, mix together the red miso, mirin, sake, sesame paste and caster sugar. Use to brush over the aubergine slices and then grill for a few more minutes. Sprinkle with poppy seeds and serve. Serve with ginger and sweet radishes.

"Due to the high level of aroma in oloroso, its taste and dryness goes perfectly with grilled aubergine mixed with red miso."

WARABIMOCHI

Best paired with:
SWEET OLOROSO,
PALE CREAM,
CREAM

THIS IS TRADITIONALLY A SUMMER DISH IN JAPAN OF MOIST, TRANSLUCENT BALLS OF bracken flour. To eat, drizzle in the thick black syrup and serve with seasonal fruit like balls of melon or grapes. Warabimochi, kinaco and mitsu can all be bought online or at good Japanese supermarkets. A smooth pale cream makes a luxurious accompaniment.

PREPARATION AND COOKING TIME: **35 MINUTES**   SERVES **5**

50 g warabimochi (bracken flour) | 500 ml cold water | 20 g icing sugar | 40 g kinaco (soya bean flour) | 100 ml mitsu (black sugar syrup) | seasonal fresh fruit, to serve

1 Mix the warabimochi with a little of the water in a pan. Stir in the remaining water to make a smooth milky liquid. Bring to the boil and simmer for 10–15 minutes, stirring continuously until the liquid becomes transparent and thick.

2 Using 2 teaspoons, scoop out little balls of the mixture and drop into cold water. Repeat until the mixture is all used up.

3 Mix together the icing sugar and the kinaco. Drain the balls very well and pat dry with an absorbent cloth. Roll the balls in the icing sugar mix and serve with drizzled mitsu (black sugar syrup) and fresh fruit.

PALE CREAM

TASTING NOTES Similarly fresh and almondy nose to fino and pale in colour, pale cream tastes almost biscuity – with a hint of pears to some. **SERVING TEMPERATURE** Well chilled – refrigerate for a good couple of hours. **FOOD** Much loved with foie gras and pâté, pale cream is also perfect for fresh fruit, light desserts and pastries.

ANTHONY FLINN

JUST TWO YEARS AFTER COMPLETING HIS STUDIES AND attaining a position at the Michelin-starred restaurant *Lords of the Manor*, Anthony Flinn moved to Spain with the intention of learning and perfecting the art of blending cultural cuisines.

After only a short time in Barcelona he gained an excellent reputation and was successful in attaining a position with Ferrán Adriá at the world-famous restaurant *El Bulli* on the Costa Brava. For the next two years he worked at *El Bulli*, the acclaimed three-Michelin-star restaurant, and it was here that he developed his love for sherry with food. He has now brought his knowledge and experience back to Leeds with *Anthony's* Restaurant.

CREAM CHEESE CANNELLONI WITH MUSCOVADO JELLY

Best paired with:
PALE CREAM,
CREAM,
PEDRO XIMÉNEZ

PEDRO XIMENEZ IS AN OBVIOUS CHOICE TO GO WITH THIS DISH AS ITS SMOOTHNESS balances with the texture of the cream cheese. It also has the same taste elements as the muscovado jelly. To make oat cookie powder simply whiz broken oat cookies in a coffee grinder until powdered. You can buy borage cress online or in organic food shops. Sheets of acetate can be bought from office or art supply shops.

PREPARATION TIME: **30 MINUTES, PLUS COOLING AND FREEZING**
COOKING TIME: **30 MINUTES**   SERVES **4**

FOR THE CREAM CHEESE CANNELLONI: 1 gelatine leaf | 65 g caster sugar | 3 egg yolks | 200 ml single cream | 200 g soft cream cheese | **FOR THE OAT CARAMEL:** 100 g fondant icing sugar | 50 g Isomalt sweetener or low calorie sweetener | 50 g liquid glucose | 40 g oat cookie powder | **FOR THE MUSCOVADO JELLY:** 100 ml cold water | 100 g light muscovado sugar | 7 g agar-agar (vegetarian gelatine) | **TO SERVE:** 1 large cucumber, peeled | a pinch of icing sugar | good quality frozen yogurt | borage cress

1 To make the cream cheese cannelloni put the gelatine leaf in cold water and soak for 5 minutes. Meanwhile, in a large bowl, whisk together the sugar and egg yolks until pale and foamy.

2 In a small pan bring the cream to the boil. While whisking, pour the hot cream over the egg yolk mixture. Drain the gelatine and whisk into the egg and cream mixture. Allow to go cold.

3 Once the cream cheese cannelloni mixture is cold whisk in the cream cheese until it leaves ribbons of mixture. Make 4 tubes from acetate and close one end of each with cling film. Pipe the mixture into the tubes and freeze for 2–4 hours until set.

4 To make the oat caramel, put the fondant sugar, sweetener and glucose in a pan and carefully bring to the boil until the temperature reaches 160°C.

5 Add the oat cookie powder and stir in quickly. Carefully pour on to a large baking tray lined with baking parchment. Allow to go cold. Preheat the oven to Gas Mark 2/150°C/300°F.

6 Break off a piece of caramel and place between 2 thin heatproof mats. Warm in the oven for a few minutes until soft. Roll the caramel out thinly and remove the top mat. Reheat the caramel a little and with your fingers pull the caramel into long, thin strands.

7 To make the muscovado jelly, gently heat the water and sugar in a pan until dissolved. Add the agar-agar and bring to the boil. Allow to go cold. Whiz the jelly with a hand blender until smooth. Chill until needed.

8 Using a potato peeler, peel long strips of cucumber and lay on cling film, slightly overlapping to create a long sheet of cucumber strips. Sprinkle the icing sugar over the cucumber.

9 Unwrap the acetate from 1 cream cheese cannelloni and place on the slices of cucumber. Roll the cucumber around the tube and trim off any excess cucumber. Repeat with the remaining cannelloni tubes.

10 To serve, drizzle the muscovado jelly on the plate, add a cannelloni, a quenelle of frozen yogurt and finish with pulled caramel and borage cress.

TIP For a simple caramel, put 125 g caster sugar in a heavy-based pan and heat over a low heat. Shake the pan gently from time to time as the sugar starts to melt. When the sugar turns to a dark caramel colour, quickly dip the base of the pan in a bowl of cold water. Immediately pour the caramel on to an oiled baking tray. Allow to go cold then break into shards.

ROAST SUCKLING PIG WITH SCALLOP RAVIOLI & BLACKBERRY SORBET

Best paired with:
PALO CORTADO,
PALE CREAM,
CREAM

A PALE CREAM SHERRY IS THE IDEAL MATCH TO COMPLEMENT THE COMBINATIONS AND flavours of this dish. It balances with the fattiness of the meat but is bold enough to challenge the acidity of the red berries. With fresh goat's cheese adding the final element it all works superbly well. For step 3, ask your butcher to vacuum-pack your saddle of pig for you.

PREPARATION TIME: **1 HOUR, PLUS FREEZING** COOKING TIME: **2 HOURS 45 MINUTES**
SERVES **4**

FOR THE BLACKBERRY SORBET: 200 g fresh blackberries | 50 ml cold water | 50 g liquid glucose | **FOR THE SUCKLING PIG:** 300 g salt | 200 g caster sugar | 100 g paprika | 1 saddle of suckling pig, boned and rolled | 100 g pork fat | **FOR THE SCALLOP RAVIOLI:** 2 king scallops | 100 g goat's cheese | 1 tablespoon chopped chives | 25 g double cream | 1 shallot, finely chopped | vanilla oil, to drizzle | **FOR THE LEMON BULGUR WHEAT:** 200 ml cold water | 200 g bulgur wheat | 25 g butter | juice of $1/2$ of a lemon | 1 tablespoon chopped chives | shelled pea's and snow pea sprouts, to serve | salt and black pepper, to season

1 For the blackberry sorbet, whiz all the ingredients together in a blender then pass through a fine sieve. Churn and freeze in an ice cream machine.

2 For the suckling pig, mix the salt, sugar and paprika together in a shallow dish. Coat the pig in the mix and leave for 45 minutes.

3 Wash off all the salt mix and vacuum-pack the pig with the pork fat. Cook the pig in a steamer at 90°C for 2 hours.

4 Meanwhile, make the scallop ravioli. Slice the scallops into 8 very thin discs. Mix the rest of the ingredients together and chill.

5 Roll the goat's cheese mix into 8 small balls and lay the scallop slices over the top of the cheese to create a ravioli shape. Chill in the fridge.

6 Preheat the oven to Gas Mark 7/220°C/425°F. Remove the pig from the vacuum pack bag and place on a roasting tray. Roast in the oven for 30–35 minutes or until golden brown and crispy.

7 Meanwhile, make the bulgur wheat. Bring the water to the boil and add the bulgur wheat. Bring back to the boil and remove from the heat. Cover completely with cling film and set aside until tender. Then stir in the butter, lemon juice, chives and season to taste.

8 To assemble, cut the suckling pig into 4. Divide the ravioli between 4 plates and drizzle each with a little of the vanilla oil over and around. Add a quenelle of blackberry sorbet or smudge lines on to each plate. Spoon on a little bulgur wheat and top with a roll of suckling pig. Garnish with snow pea sprouts, shelled peas and the juices from the suckling pig.

TIP To make your own vanilla oil gently warm 200 ml rapeseed oil. Remove from the heat. Split 4 vanilla pods in half and remove the seeds and add to the oil. Chop the leftover vanilla pods into small pieces and add to the oil. Leave to infuse for at least 12 hours. Store in the fridge for up to 3 months.

JOHN DORY WITH PARSNIP PURÉE & COCKEREL'S CREST

Best paired with:
MANZANILLA,
PALO CORTADO

THE FRESHNESS OF WHITE JOHN DORY FILLETS COMBINES PERFECTLY WITH A CRISP, fresh manzanilla, which also complements the fattiness of the crispy chicken skin perfectly by balancing the palate. Cockerel's crest can be ordered from good butchers or online.

PREPARATION TIME: **15 MINUTES, PLUS 10 HOURS CHILLING**
COOKING TIME: **3 HOURS 15 MINUTES**   SERVES **4**

4 cockerels' crests | skins from 4 chicken breasts | 200 g duck fat | 200 g parsnips, peeled, trimmed and cut into chunks | 200 ml milk | 2 tablespoons single cream | 200 g pistachios | 2 tablespoons pistachio oil | 2 tablespoons olive oil | 2 x 750 g John Dory, cleaned and filleted | salt, to sprinkle and season | cubes of apple dusted in grated pistachio nuts, to serve

1 The day before, prepare the cockerels' crests. Plunge the crests in boiling water for 1–2 minutes. Remove with a slotted spoon and refresh in iced water.

2 Pat the crests dry then remove the membrane and sprinkle salt all over the cockerels' crests and leave in the fridge for 10 hours.

3 The next day preheat the oven to Gas Mark 1/140°C/275°F. Lay the chicken skins out over a cooling wire on top of a baking tray and bake in the oven for 40 minutes until golden brown and crispy. Sprinkle with salt and set aside.

4 Decrease the oven to Gas Mark $^1/_2$/130°C/250°F. Wash the salt off the crests and place them in a roasting tray with the duck fat. Cook in the oven for $2^1/_2$ hours.

5 Meanwhile, make the parsnip purée. Put the parsnips in a pan with the milk and bring to the boil. Cook on a low heat for 15–20 minutes until tender. Drain and cool slightly.

6 Put the parsnips into a food processor with the cream and whiz until smooth. Season to taste with salt. Pass through a fine sieve to remove any lumps. Set aside.

7 Meanwhile, make the pistachio praline. Whiz the pistachios and the oil in a mini food processor until smooth. Pass through a sieve, add a pinch of salt and chill quickly to retain the green colour.

8 To assemble, heat the olive oil in a frying pan and pan-fry the John Dory for 3–4 minutes on each side. Drizzle some of the praline and purée over each plate and arrange the apple, crispy chicken skin, cockerel's crest and fish on top. Drizzle with pan juices and serve.

"The freshness of white John Dory fillets combines with this style of sherry. Being a crisp, fresh sherry manzanilla complements the fattiness of the crispy chicken skin perfectly by balancing the palate."

CURED DUCK BREAST WITH PRUNE PURÉE

Best paired with:
OLOROSO,
PALO CORTADO,
CREAM

THIS HOME CURED DUCK IS A RICH BUT EXTREMELY SWEET RED MEAT THAT WORKS fantastically well with the deep flavours of oloroso. They both have a smoky aroma and flavour that blends perfectly together. For step 4, ask your butcher to vacuum-pack the duck breasts for you. You could buy ready-made confit duck (a 750g jar will give you two duck legs).

PREPARATION TIME: 45 MINUTES, PLUS 14 HOURS CHILLING
COOKING TIME: 3 HOURS 40 MINUTES   SERVES 4

2 duck breasts, skin removed and reserved | 100 g curing salt | 100 g caster sugar | 500 ml cold water | 200 g good quality sea salt | 6 star anise | 7 g pink peppercorns | 6 crushed black cardamoms pods | 2 tablespoons vanilla oil (page 130) | FOR THE DUCK CONFIT: 2 duck legs | 300 g duck fat | macadamia nuts, grated, to serve | FOR THE PRUNE PURÉE: 1 small vanilla pod | 200 g ready-to-eat prunes | 3 tablespoons cold water | FOR THE PICKLED PINK SHALLOTS: 12 pink shallots, peeled | 100 g white wine vinegar | 3 tablespoons cold water | 25 g caster sugar | snow pea shoots, purple shizo, shelled peas and grapefruit flesh, to serve

1 Cover the duck breasts with curing salt and leave for 2 hours in the fridge to cure. Wash off all the curing salt with fresh cold water.

2 Mix together the sugar, water, sea salt, star anise, peppercorns and cardamoms in a bowl and add the cured duck breasts. Cover and chill in the fridge for 12 hours. Remove the duck from the brine and wash again under cold water.

3 Meanwhile make the confit of duck. Preheat the oven to Gas Mark $^1/_2$/130°C/250°F. Put the duck legs in a roasting pan with the duck fat and cook for 3 hours. Once cooked remove the meat from the duck legs while warm and lay on cling film. Then roll into a tube and chill.

4 Meanwhile, vacuum-pack the breasts with the vanilla oil and seal. Cook the duck breasts in a steamer at 650°C for approximately 2 hours or until the core temperature is 630°C. Chill. It is really important that the temperature is controlled.

5 Preheat the oven to Gas Mark 1/140°C/275°F. Lay out the reserved duck skin over a cooling wire on top of a baking tray and bake in the oven for 40 minutes until golden brown and crispy. Sprinkle with sea salt.

6 Meanwhile, make the prune purée. Split the vanilla pod and remove the seeds. Put the seeds in a pan with the prunes and water and bring to the boil. Rapidly boil until the liquid is reduced by half. Whiz until smooth. Chill.

7 Mix all of the ingredients together for the pickled shallots and put into a pan. Bring to the boil then remove from the heat.

8 To assemble, slice the duck into thin slices and divide between 4 plates. Cut the tube of confit duck in to 1 cm lengths and roll in the macadamia nuts and place on the sliced duck. Top with prune purée and duck skin. Scatter over the pickled shallots and finish with the snow pea shoots, purple shizo, shelled peas and grapefruit flesh to serve.

MILK POT

A LIGHT AND FRESH FINO SHERRY REALLY BALANCES WITH THE CREAMY FLAVOURS AND textures of this complex combination. Its freshness balances the richness of the dish and does not compete or overpower the numerous flavours; in fact its fruitiness complements the dish. Equally, sweeter styles of sherry go wonderfully well with this dish.

PREPARATION TIME: **1 HOUR, PLUS FREEZING AND INFUSING** COOKING TIME: **3 HOURS** SERVES **4**

4 x cream cheese cannelloni, see Cream Cheese Cannelloni with Muscovado Jelly, page 128 | good quality frozen yogurt and powdered oat cookies, to serve | **FOR THE VANILLA FOAM AND TIGER NUT MILK:** 200 g tiger nuts | 200 ml cold water | 2 vanilla pods | 200 ml full fat milk | 40 g caster sugar | **FOR THE MILK CARAMEL:** 100 g fondant icing sugar | 50 g liquid glucose | 50 g Isomalt sweetener or low calorie sweetener | 50 g milk powder | **FOR THE MILK JELLY:** 200 g full fat milk | 50 g caster sugar | 7 g agar agar (vegetarian gelatine) | **FOR THE MILK RAVIOLI:** 395 g can condensed milk | 500 ml full fat milk | 100 g single cream | **FOR THE CHILLED RICE PUDDING:** 250 g pudding rice | 500 ml full fat milk | 100 g caster sugar | 100 g double cream

1 To make the tiger nut milk, whiz the nuts and water to a paste and leave to infuse in the fridge for 24 hours. Pass through a fine sieve to remove the milky water. Chill in the fridge.

2 To make the milk caramel, put the fondant sugar, glucose and sweetener in a pan and carefully bring to the boil until the temperature reaches 160°C.

3 Add the milk powder and stir in quickly. Carefully pour on to a large baking tray lined with baking parchment. Allow to go cold. Preheat the oven to Gas Mark 2/150°C/300°F.

4 Break off a piece of caramel and place between 2 thin heatproof mats. Warm in the oven for a few minutes until soft. Remove the top mat and roll the caramel out thinly. Reheat the caramel a little and, with your fingers, pull the caramel into long, thin strands.

5 To make the milk jelly, bring all the ingredients to the boil in a pan. Pour into a bowl and chill in the fridge until set. Then break up with a fork.

6 To make the milk ravoli, place the can of condensed milk in a large pan of water and boil for 3 hours. Allow to go cold.

7 Meanwhile, mix all the rice pudding ingredients in a pan and cook slowly on a low heat until the rice is soft and has soaked up the milk and cream. Chill in the fridge.

8 Then, for the ravioli, place the milk in a large pan and heat to 80°C and leave at this temperature for 15–20 minutes until it has formed a skin. Paint some cling film with the cream. Lift the skin off the milk and lay over the cream. Paint the top side with cream and chill.

9 Once cold cut the skin into 4 squares, spoon on a ball of the condensed milk and fold the edges over to form a ravioli, paint with more cream and chill.

10 For the vanilla foam, split the vanilla pods in half. Remove the seeds and place in a pan with the pod, milk and sugar. Bring to the boil and then remove from the heat and leave to cool. Remove the pod and chill in the fridge.

11 To assemble, unwrap the cream cheese rolls from the acetate and roll in the powdered oat cookies. Aerate the vanilla foam with a hand held blender. Arrange all the elements of the dish on the plate and finish with the vanilla foam and smudge the frozen yoghurt around.

IN JANUARY 2001, SHANE OSBORN AGED JUST 29, BECAME the very first Australian to attain Michelin status. Born and bought up in Perth, Australia, Shane has worked in Europe for the past ten years. He became head chef at *Pied à Terre* in 1999 progressing to joint owner with business partner David Moore. Since then Shane has taken *Pied à Terre* from strength to strength, having managed to retain their first Michelin star he then celebrated even greater success with the return of their second in January 2003.

"There are so many different varieties: like different types of wine."

Shane considers sherry the perfect drink for summer and is keen for it to shed its old-fashioned image. Although his food does not have a particularly Spanish influence he frequently recommends sherry as the perfect match for his dishes, particularly his tasting menus.

BITTER SWEET CHOCOLATE TARTLETS WITH CARAMELISED HAZELNUTS

Best paired with:
MEDIUM,
CREAM,
PEDRO XIMÉNEZ

THESE TINY LITTLE MOUTHFULS ARE A CHOCOHOLIC'S HEAVEN AND ARE THE PERFECT companion to a glass of Pedro Ximénez. To blind bake, line each tartlet pastry case with a square of baking parchment and fill with baking beans or dried pulses. Remove the parchment to cool.

PREPARATION TIME: **20 MINUTES, PLUS 1 HOUR RESTING** COOKING TIME: **30 MINUTES**
MAKES **12**

250 g plain flour | 10 g cocoa powder | 115g caster sugar | pinch of salt | 125 g butter | 2 eggs, beaten in separate bowls | 80 ml milk | 125 ml double cream | 200 g dark bitter chocolate, broken into pieces | 10 g liquid glucose | 2 tablespoons water | 12 hazelnuts

1 To make the pastry, sieve the flour, cocoa, 1 tablespoon sugar and salt into a bowl. Rub in the butter using your fingertips until it resembles fine breadcrumbs.

2 Stir in 1 beaten egg and 1 teaspoon milk to form a soft dough, adding a little more milk if the mixture is too dry. Leave to rest for at least an hour.

3 Preheat the oven to Gas Mark 4/180°C/350°F and grease twelve 3 cm tartlet cases. Roll out the pastry on a lightly floured surface until 3 mm thick. Use to line the prepared tartlet cases and blind bake in the oven for 12 minutes. Allow to cool.

4 Meanwhile, reduce the oven temperature to Gas Mark 1/2/120°C/250°F. Put the double cream and remaining milk in a pan and bring to the boil.

5 Pour on to the chocolate and gently stir until completely melted and combined. Allow to cool slightly and then stir in the remaining egg. Use to fill the cases then bake for 18–20 minutes.

6 Meanwhile, put the remaining caster sugar, glucose and water in a pan and cook gently until the sugar dissolves. Pour on to an oiled baking tray and allow to cool. Break up and whiz in a food processor until powdered. Put into a bowl.

7 Heat a pan until hot and dry-fry the hazelnuts until golden brown all over, shaking the pan continuously. Immediately drop into the caramel powder, shake off any excess and allow to cool. Use to decorate each tart.

MEDIUM

TASTING NOTES Medium is actually a sweetened oloroso. Amber to mahogany in colour, with a fragrant walnutty nose, expect a sweet taste with swirls of caramel. **SERVING TEMPERATURE** Lightly chilled or as a warming aperitif. **FOOD** Fantastic with desserts, pâté or quiches.

PARKINSON'S APPEAL

IN ORDER TO SUPPORT FUNDRAISING FOR DEEP BRAIN stimulation, a groundbreaking approach to Parkinson's Disease, all the chef contributors to *The Perfect Marriage* have generously agreed to donate their royalty fees to The Parkinson's Appeal.

"It's very strange being diagnosed with Parkinson's Disease: it's one of those things you think other people get, but this time I got it.

Luckily I had my usual cure for tricky situations, a good lunch and a few glasses of wine to throw things into perspective. Unfortunately as the Parkinson's took more of a hold my precious lunch became a battle with the tablecloth, the table, my chair, flailing cutlery and, depending on the violence of the twitch, food could be propelled into the air.

Then I was accorded a miracle in my own lunchtime. I had deep brain stimulation (DBS), performed on me by a team of unbelievably dedicated angels at Queen Square Hospital of Neurology. This is the unit that Parkinson's Appeal are raising funds for, the total of which will be met by the NHS, thus securing the future of this innovative and amazing team, and offering hope to many others who, like me, may have thought they had indulged in their favourite pastime for the last time.

DBS can offer a whole new lease of life, which my growing tummy is a testament to. So I raise my glass to Parkinson's Appeal."

Fergus Henderson

THE PARKINSON'S APPEAL
FOR DEEP BRAIN STIMULATION